A RICH DAD LI
with Fore

THE
ART OF
COMMERCIAL
REAL ESTATE
LEASING

HOW TO LEASE A COMMERCIAL BUILDING
AND KEEP IT LEASED

R. CRAIG COPPOLA, CRE, SIOR, CCIM

Published by Rich Dad Library
an imprint of RDA Press, LLC

Any registered trademarks referenced in this book are the property of their respective owners.

RDA Press LLC
15170 N. Hayden Road
Scottsdale, AZ 85260
480-998-5400
Visit our Web sites: RDAPress.com and RichDadLibrary.com

Printed in the United States of America

First Edition: October 2014

ISBN: 978-0-9911104-2-1

DEDICATION

To Andrew Cheney, my partner and

friend. To my partners at Lee & Associates

for their support and expertise. Starting

Lee & Associates Arizona with my

partners has been the best business

decision I have made.

Acknowledgments

There are several people who deserve thanks and more for the creation of this book. Specifically, I would like to thank Jake Johnson for helping me with the writing and the thousands of clients who have made my career.

CONTENTS

FOREWORD

In 1991, I recruited an incredibly smart and business-savvy man named Craig Coppola to help open the Phoenix office of Lee & Associates. At the time, Lee & Associates already had several high-functioning offices, and we were expanding to new markets outside of California with new talent to lead the way. Craig was finishing his MBA, was an incredible forward-thinker with great vision not only for the Phoenix office, but for that segment of industry, identifying the coming of structural changes before they happened.

In all the years since, I have watched Craig grow to become the top office producer in Lee & Associates history, winning highly-coveted awards like Broker of the Year, time and time again. He remains Lee's Top Producing Office Broker in the company's history, an honor that has been earned over years of making transactions. If anyone knows the ins and outs of real estate and the fine art of negotiating a lease, it's him.

I've seen his talents at work, capitalizing on a successful personal investment history to build a business profile, while also challenging and living life to the fullest in his participation of physical feats such as hiking, marathons, and Tae Kwon Do. Having an entire book dedicated to leasing shows just how much focus Craig gives the little things, and I have no doubt that anyone looking to master this part of a transaction will learn all they need to know from this book.

— Bill Lee
Founder of Lee & Associates

INTRODUCTION

THE ART OF LEASING

Have you ever heard this one? You can't make money as an artist.

In my experience, people who have a limited view of art say that. Sure, it can be tough to make a living as a painter or a writer, and if you want to be a musician, you'll probably spend your life eking out a meager living playing from venue to venue. Very few artists in those types of fields have the necessary combination of talent, drive, tenacity, and savvy to become a major success. However, to me there are many kinds of art.

I played baseball for many years, including getting drafted and playing with the Minnesota Twins organization. Naturally, I'm a big fan of the sport. Baseball is art. As stated by journalist George F. Will, "Baseball, it is said, is only a game. True. And the Grand Canyon is only a hole in Arizona." There's something amazing about a perfectly-thrown fastball that's down and away; something grand about a game-winning base hit. As everybody knows, major league baseball players aren't hurting for money. They're artists who make a great living.

Everyone can learn how to throw a ball or swing a bat, but only a few perfect it. What separates professional baseball players from wannabes?

THE DIVIDING LINE

Many people mistakenly believe those who master the art of anything are successful only because they have natural ability. However, the dividing line between average and excellent has less to do with natural talent and genetics and more to do with passion, tenacity, and commitment.

Daniel Coyle, in his book *The Talent Code*, dismantled the myth that great talent is born and showed how *anyone* can master *anything* by practicing consistently and methodically, what he calls "deep practice." In the book, he writes, "Our intuition tells us that practice relates to talent in the same way that a whetstone relates to a knife: it's vital but useless without a solid blade of so-called natural ability. Deep practice raises an intriguing possibility: that practice might be the way to forge the blade itself."

Coyle breaks deep practice down into three rules:

Practice Skills in Chunks: Visualize what success looks like and then break that down into manageable chunks, practicing each chunk slowly and methodically, until you master it.

Use Repetition: Practice often and consistently, never letting up. Mastering a skill could take as long as ten years, which requires incredible tenacity.

Learn to Feel Mistakes: As you practice each skill chunk, you must identify when you're making a mistake, correct that mistake, and learn from it, just as a baby learns how to walk from falling.

What this means is, anyone can take knowledge and apply it in awesome and inspiring ways to master whatever they're passionate about. Anyone can become an artist—a true master—in his or her chosen field. The reality is that only a small minority have the work ethic required to do so.

THE ART OF LEASING

Why am I starting a book on commercial real estate leasing with a discussion on art? Because I believe that, while there is a science to leasing, there is a lot more art to it. There are plenty of men and women out there who know how to lease a building. They understand the mechanics—and their approach is mechanical as a result. They make a good living. They pull decent deals together. They aspire to build a modest portfolio. They're not *unhappy* with their investments.

But there are others who understand that leasing is an art form that requires constant, deep practice to perfect. Not only do they have a solid grasp of the mechanics of leasing, but they also have the passion, tenacity, and commitment to take them to the next level. They don't just make a good living; they make a *great* one. They don't just pull together decent deals; they set the standard for deal making. They don't settle for a modest portfolio; they build a stellar one and are *extremely* happy with their investments.

Over 3,300 transactions deep into my career, I have created this tried and true formula for winning the leasing game. This process will show you how to maximize your value/return, no matter what the market, no matter what the product type.

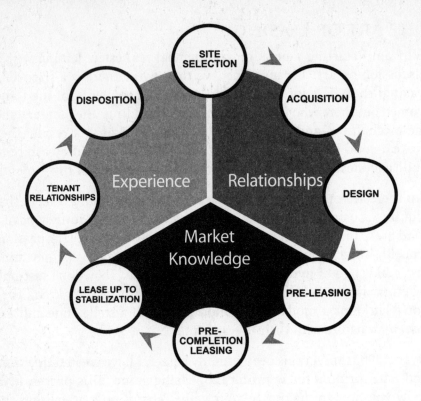

NO SUCH THING AS AN OVERNIGHT SUCCESS

I can say confidently that, in my experience, the difference between practitioners and artists is passion, tenacity, and commitment. The people who are successful, who rise to the top of their game, are the ones who care the most, practice the most, learn the most, and throw their whole existence into their passions. Sure, there are always natural talents, those who make incredibly skilled and hard tasks look simple and effortless—but those types of people are extremely rare. For the most part, people are on equal footing in terms of intelligence and ability. So, in the end, it's those who want it the most who succeed and those who care the most who create great art.

There's no such thing as an overnight success. Just because you've never heard of them before does not mean the stars, the headliners, have come out of nowhere. Anyone successful has worked many years, poured themselves into learning and practicing for hours every day, and been tenacious enough to take life's setbacks and failures and use them to fuel forward. That is a mindset that can't be taught. It must be developed.

IN IT TO WIN IT

My first book, *How to Win in Commercial Real Estate Investing*, was subtitled *Find, Evaluate & Purchase Your First Commercial Property in 9 Weeks or Less*. In that book, I laid out a nine-week, highly intensive program designed to create the type of passion, commitment, and tenacity required to be a successful real estate investor. Basically, it was a "no wimps allowed" book.

The thinking behind that book was that there were already a lot of books that gave you the *knowledge* needed to invest in commercial real estate, but there weren't any books that forced you to apply that knowledge. I purposely wrote a book that needed to be practiced to be useful. I did this because I care that you actually become successful, that you actually become a real estate investor—not just someone who says, "Yeah, I read that book."

The nine-week program was, essentially, a boot camp for real estate investing, taking the concept of deep practice and breaking down the components of successful real estate investing. Each week built on the previous one.

Week 1: Focus Your Goals

Week 2: Learn Your Local Real Estate Landscape

Week 3: Exploring the Fundamentals

Weeks 4 and 5: Advanced Research

Week 6: Find the Money

Week 7: Narrow Your Options and Pick the Winners

Weeks 8 and 9: Make an Offer and Negotiate the Deal

By the end of the nine-week program, you've not only learned everything you need to know about purchasing commercial real estate, but also actually put into practice everything you need to find, value, buy, and lease a property.

My mindset when writing the book was to speak to readers who were "in it to win it." Because if there's one thing I can't stand, it's people who do things half-heartedly. I don't live my life that way, and I expect that people who are serious about real estate won't either. Otherwise, what's the point? Isn't it just a waste of time?

BUYING VS. LEASING

The reason I was able to create a nine-week program for real estate investing success in my earlier book is because finding, valuing, and buying a property is a fairly scientific process. There are certain fundamentals that can be learned and applied quickly. Anyone can do it.

But finding, valuing, and buying a property is only half the battle. You can have the greatest portfolio of commercial real estate properties in the world, but if you can't lease that portfolio, it's worthless. It's the lease that creates the ultimate value of a property. Why? The lease creates cash flow, and cash flow is what gives your property its true value. A lot of people will say you make your money at the buy. I say you make your money at the lease. I have a client that was paying $29 per square foot for rent. When we finished negotiations on a renewal, their rent for the next twelve years was going to be lower in the twelfth year of the renewal than what the client was paying at the time of renewal. Yes, I say you make your money at the lease.

Executing a good lease isn't just a scientific process—it's also an art that requires much practice.

ASSET VS. LIABILITY

This is a good opportunity to talk about cash flow. For some of you, this may be a refresher. For others, it may be a revelation.

In *Rich Dad Poor Dad*, my friend and business partner Robert Kiyosaki gave a very simple definition of an asset and a liability. An *asset*, he said, is something that puts money in your pocket, and a *liability* is something that takes money out of your pocket.

This is different from the traditional definition of assets used by accountants. That's because accountants use an asset's assumed market value and apply it to your net worth - but net worth is worthless. Why? Markets change. In the end, the only thing that makes an investment worth its salt is steady cash flowing into your pocket every month. The only way you can achieve that in commercial real estate is through a lease. The most beautiful, well-located building in the world is a worthless liability if you can't lease it.

An unleased building takes money out of your pocket instead of putting money in it. The lease you put on your property is what makes it an asset because the lease determines how much money you will earn each month to counteract your operating expenses. The better the lease, the better the cash flow. The better the cash flow, the better the asset—and the more valuable it will be.

LEASING TAKES ART

While my first book had a chapter on leasing, it was really more of an overview. The reality is, you can't do justice to the art of leasing in a single chapter. It became apparent to me that I needed to write a book solely on the topic of leasing. This is that book. Leasing is my passion.

In my research, I found there are many books that teach the fundamentals of putting together a lease or that can help you understand the legal implications and terms of a lease. Those books primarily focus on the mechanics of leasing. However, I couldn't find a single book that focused on the art of leasing—the marketing savvy, the sales skills, and the intuitive knowledge needed to maximize the potential of your properties through leasing.

Traditionally, most real estate books—my first book included—focus on investment and ownership. There are some excellent books on those subjects. Other books, like my friend Ken McElroy's book *The ABCs of Property Management*, focus on managing your property well.

Those books mention leasing and spend some time on the subject, but there is no book focused solely on leasing as part of your investment strategy. To me, this is a gaping hole in real estate education.

LEASING IS A LOT OF WORK

I think the reason there aren't many books on leasing is that leasing is a lot of work. For the most part, successful leasing professionals spend years and years honing their craft and learning on the job. It takes lots of trial and error to master the art of leasing.

For instance, my company, Lee & Associates, has a training program for potential leasing agents, a position called "Runner."

The Runner program is an intensive training period broken into three steps over 36 months (yes, three years!) that train the Runner to interact with clients, research markets, tour clients, oversee billing, practice cold calling, and understand industry-standard software. It's not for the faint of heart.

STEP 1:
TRAINING (6 MONTHS)

The Runner spends a high percentage of time transitioning from research to client interaction. He or she spends progressively more time working with clients and landlords in the form of meetings and tours, and also spends a lot of time researching office listings, learning the overall market, each individual sub-market, and the specific buildings located in those markets.

STEP 2:
FORMAL SALES TRAINING (24 MONTHS)

Over the next 24 months, the Runner makes the transition to transaction-oriented training and begins working with the Principal Brokerage Team to increase productivity by helping take on smaller clients and spending more time with clients in the field. Additionally, the Runner begins leading transactions and cold calling potential clients.

STEP 3:
JUNIOR PARTNERSHIP RELATIONSHIP
(6 MONTHS)

By the time our runner hits this stage, they have worked 80 hours a week for over two years. They sit in the same cubicle with our whole team and they have been to meeting after meeting, tour after tour, negotiation after negotiation. They literally have thousands of different nuances and market information they have acquired along the way. They are ready to compete.

The purpose of telling you about our program isn't to discourage you. It's to encourage you.

Here's the deal: You don't learn the art of leasing in a school or even in a book (sorry to disappoint you). You learn it by practicing it, and anyone, including you, can put in the time and effort required. The question is, will you?

WHAT THIS BOOK IS AND ISN'T

This book serves to fill the void in the vast amount of commercial real estate books available by focusing on leasing—and only leasing. Through this book you'll learn:

- What leasing is and why it's important.
- How to position your building to be as attractive as possible.
- Why leasing really is marketing.
- How to be a better salesperson.
- The skills required to negotiate leases and evaluate offers.
- How to find and partner with the best team members.

Additionally, this book will teach you some of the technical terms and legal items necessary to be successful.

At the end of your read, you'll have a great foundation for understanding the how and why of leasing. But it will take hard work and trial and error for you to discover the art of commercial real estate leasing.

So, this book isn't going to make you a master. That will take years of hard work. That being said, this book *will* give you the foundational information and inspiration needed to spend a lifetime mastering the art of commercial real estate leasing—and it will take a lifetime. But if you put in the time and effort required to become a great artist, you'll reap huge dividends professionally, personally, and financially. And you'll be one of those few artists who create great work and make a great living.

As Michelangelo said, "Genius is eternal patience."

Let's get started.

CHAPTER 1

WHAT IS LEASING, AND WHY IS IT IMPORTANT?

Most people's first experience with leasing is when they move out of their parents' house and get their first apartment. I remember as a young man the experience of touring various places where I might live on my own for the first time. There was a mixture of fear and excitement. I wanted the right place where I could have a good time with my friends, feel at home, and maybe even impress a girl.

My first apartment was like most freshly-minted college graduates without ANY money. Yes, we had the foil on the cardboard covering the window so no light or heat would get in. Remember, Phoenix in the summer is hot. The place was a converted hotel. We got to walk down the corridor, into our apartment. We had used furniture, including beds. But it was ours.

For the most part, finding an apartment was a one-way transaction. Sure, I was in control of where I wanted to rent, but once I decided, the landlord was in the driver's seat. He set the terms and I signed the paper. It didn't really matter—I was just happy to have a place of my own.

My first apartment lease was only a couple of pages long. It had a few pertinent details like the date, term of the rental period, monthly rent, and policies and fees for getting into the place, for late rent, and for getting out. (I should have read them better, too. I lost my keys and had a number of costs I didn't expect when I moved out!) It was a simple document. More than likely, it was the same lease everyone else in the apartment community signed.

Chances are I just described the leasing experience most people picking up this book have had—including you.

Some of you might have even been on the other side. You might have been or are now landlords. Maybe you own a couple of houses or a small apartment building. So you know a little bit more about the complexities of leasing. You know it takes some time and money to find the right cash-flowing property. It's also work to maintain the building and to market it well to find the right tenants.

For the most part, however, the process is relatively simple. You want a good complex, in a good location, and you want to attract good tenants. Your lawyer might have helped you draft a decent lease that you use for every tenant—or maybe you found one on the local multi-housing association website—and your leases turn over every six to eighteen months, on average.

This type of leasing is what is known as residential real estate leasing—and it has in no way prepared you for commercial real estate leasing.

EVEN THE 'PROS' HAVE A LOT TO LEARN

My good friends Robert and Kim Kiyosaki are successful investors and financial educators. Many people know them as savvy commercial real estate investors—and they are. For much of their investing career, however, they were involved in residential real estate through houses and apartments.

I remember the first time Robert and Kim came to me with a potential commercial real estate deal. They were interested in an office building. At a casual glance, it seemed like a good deal. The building was nice—

"cute," as Kim said—well maintained, and in a good area. I didn't pay much attention to the building or the location. I just looked at the parking lot.

The zoning laws in the city in which they were considering buying had changed in the 1980s, after the building was built. I knew just from looking at the parking lot that the deal was a bad one. The building would never lease up because there weren't enough parking stalls. When the building was just 70 percent leased, a hundred percent of the parking lot would be spoken for.

Secondly, I told them that a "cute" building usually attracted "cute" businesses, which usually were non-credit businesses. Instead, I encouraged them to find a solid, "boring" building that would attract a different type of tenant, one that was a well-run, solid-credit business. This is because, in commercial real estate, you're stuck with your tenant for years, and it's important to know they'll be in business for a while.

All this is to say that even for the most seasoned investors, commercial real estate is a different game with a high learning curve. In commercial real estate, the value of a building is based on the leases, and the leases are based on the type of tenant you can attract, which is based on factors such as location, access, parking, aesthetics, zoning, and more.

Today, Robert and Kim are fantastic commercial real estate investors. It took a lot of diligence and a huge investment in their financial education to get to that point.

RESIDENTIAL VS. COMMERCIAL LEASING

The residential leasing process is a fairly simple one. Generally, you place an ad in the paper, put a sign in the lawn, and show your property to prospective tenants. If someone is interested, you have them fill out a standard application, run a basic credit check, follow up on references, and verify income and employment. If it all checks out, you approve the tenant, and they move in.

As mentioned earlier, the residential lease is usually a simple one and is pretty standard no matter what market you're in. The lease terms for residential real estate are short, lasting on average six to eighteen months.

Most residential leases have provisions for either the tenant or the landlord to cover utilities and minor upgrades and fixes to the interiors, and the landlord covers such things as insurance and taxes for the structure, with the tenant finding insurance to cover personal belongings.

Commercial leasing, on the other hand, is very complex. For instance, the type of lease used can vary significantly. There are few "standard" lease forms, and there are at least four common types of leases. Here are the main four types of leases, but there are other variations:

Gross: This is a full-service lease. In a gross lease, the landlord pays for all utilities, the upkeep of the building, and the maintenance costs. The tenant pays for everything in one check to the owner. Admittedly, this is a simplistic definition, as these leases have escalation clauses for overages, but we will review that later.

Net: While there are some nuances to the term "net," it generally means that the tenant directly pays for portions of the costs associated with the property's utilities, upkeep, and maintenance. So, for example, if you have a net-utilities lease, the tenant pays directly for utilities.

Triple Net: This is a popular term and lease for investors looking for a simple return. In a Triple Net, or NNN lease, the owner receives a base rent check and is only responsible for the structure and capital elements of the property, such as the roof, parking lot, and more. The tenant covers all other expenses included in the operation of the building, such as utilities, taxes, maintenance, and more. Generally, you find these types of leases for businesses in retail, such as fast-food franchises, drug stores, and warehouses.

Absolute Triple Net: In an Absolute Triple Net lease, the tenant pays for everything. This type of lease is mostly used for single-tenant properties, and these assets provide little work for the landlord. The landlord also gives up a lot of control of the asset. Like everything, there are trade-offs for this type of lease.

Besides different types of leases, there are also regional differences that affect leasing markets. So, in addition to having a general knowledge of commercial leasing, you also have to work toward being an expert in your region; and within that region, you have to know the differences in sub-markets.

In New York City, for instance, leases are almost always Triple Net. In West Coast markets, they're generally Gross leases. That doesn't mean that even in these regions there aren't differences. In some states, there might be a different type of lease from that in another state of the same region. Even in the same building, there might be different types of leases. New owners change leases all the time.

In addition to market differences, there are also structural differences. The reality is, the term "commercial leasing" is broad and a bit misleading. A casual observer would think commercial leasing is a coherent concept, but it's really multifaceted, made up of industrial, retail, shopping center, office building, hospitality, land leases, and more—all under the umbrella of the term "commercial leasing." Within development of the property, there are different classes of buildings, such as A, B, and C properties.

Each one of these classes has its own culture and way of doing things. Unlike residential leasing, every one of these property types usually involves long-term leases that span years. So, finding the right match for your property is just as important—if not more so—than actually renting the property. That means you have to know how to find, attract, and retain quality tenants, and you have to know when a tenant, even though he or she might be qualified, isn't the right fit for your property and your investment needs. This book will discuss all those concepts in depth.

The point is, in residential leasing it's generally one size fits all. That's not the case with commercial leasing. Rather, commercial leasing is like a custom-tailored suit, and if you don't know what you're doing, you can make some big mistakes that will cost you a lot of time and money.

NEGOTIATION SKILLS

In commercial leasing, the skill of negotiation is incredibly important, and that's why there are brokers who specialize in marketing and negotiating commercial properties. In reality, there are actually two sets of negotiations. You first come to the terms—often in what is known as a Letter of Intent (LOI)—and then you negotiate the lease.

Both the landlord and the potential tenant come to the table with needs and preferences. The landlord is looking for a good fit and a good return. The potential tenant is likewise looking for a good fit and for a lease that will fit well with his or her business plan. Unlike residential leasing, because there are so many variables, the potential tenant has a lot of pull to make adjustments and negotiate the terms of the lease. If you try to make a change on a residential lease, you'll get laughed out of the building. With commercial leasing, negotiation is the norm.

Negotiation of commercial lease terms is very technical and requires navigating a host of legal points and issues. As such, they usually involve qualified brokers.

Here are just a handful of items that are negotiated in an LOI for a commercial lease:

Rent: Unlike residential leasing, the going market rate is hard to pin down in a given market. Within regions, cities, sub-markets, and even within buildings, leasing rates can vary and are negotiated based on the market conditions, the needs of the landlord and the tenant, and the other provisions in the lease. Additionally, because commercial leases span for a much longer term than residential leases, there are often negotiated provisions for rent escalations over the term of the lease. Expect back-and-forth discussions on the leasing rate, terms, and concessions in negotiations with potential tenants.

Term: In commercial leasing, the term of the lease can last anywhere from one year to decades. Additionally, the negotiations of the terms will determine the commencement date of the lease. In residential leasing, the tenant usually takes possession the month after the lease signing, or sooner. In commercial leasing, it is, on average, ninety days before the tenant even takes possession—and sometimes longer, depending on improvements and the needs of the tenant. For instance, I recently completed a deal where the tenant didn't move in for seventeen months.

Taxes: Who will pay the taxes? Which ones? How will they be pro-rated? Each one of these things will be up for negotiation during the Letter of Intent (LOI) phase. There are different kinds of taxes: property, rental, association dues, and more.

Utilities: Likewise, who will pay for the utilities? Which ones? How will they be calculated? Who is responsible for making sure they are connected and working properly? All of these issues are negotiated and vary depending on the market.

Security Deposit: Think of the security deposit like insurance. It protects the landlord's investment should the tenant damage the property. This, too, is negotiable on every lease.

Tenant Improvements (TI): In residential leasing, each unit generally comes as is. Sure, you have to replace a broken appliance, paint the walls, and replace carpets. Structurally, the units stay the same for everyone. In commercial leasing, each space is usually unique and is catered to the needs of the tenant. Often, a landlord is responsible for helping the prospective tenant with improvements to the space, or TIs. These can be costly and are negotiated at the lease negotiation phase. The amount a landlord pays depends on the need to rent the space and trends in the property's market.

That being said, one growing trend in the past couple of cycles is "spec" suites where the landlord builds out suites generally and the tenant agrees to rent the space as is. Owners are trying to cut down the on-going cost of tenant rollover, which in commercial leasing can be very expensive.

Common Areas: Every property has common areas such as courtyards, lobbies, restrooms, and more that need to be maintained. Will the landlord maintain these? Or will that be the responsibility of the tenant? Who will pay the common-area utility costs? How about improvements to the common areas—who pays for those? Who will maintain the parking lots? The signage? These are all negotiable items.

Insurance: In residential leasing, the landlord, generally, is expected to obtain insurance for the structures and make sure the investment is adequately covered. The tenant is responsible for making sure the personal effects of the unit are covered. In commercial leasing, these items are negotiable. Again, who pays for the insurance is a matter of the prevailing market conditions and the regional considerations.

Parking: Residential units need only one or two parking spaces per unit. In commercial leasing, parking is a big deal because businesses need places for their employees and customers to park. Parking includes the ratio (how many stalls per square foot leased) and the cost of the stalls, usually charged as a monthly fee. Parking issues can make or break a good deal and are a matter of negotiation.

Additional negotiations include concessions like free rent, security, moving allowances, signage rights—you might not want your building to look like a billboard—and hours of operation, as some businesses work around the clock and cost the landlord a fortune in utilities.

COMMERCIAL LEASING IS LIKE A MARRIAGE

When I was single and looking for someone to spend my life with, I knew exactly what I was looking for. I wanted to meet a woman who was smart, attractive, independent, strong, funny, and fun—and I was picky.

I knew that marrying the wrong woman would be a bad decision with horrible consequences. Therefore, I wanted to make sure I found the right one. Thankfully, I did, and I've been happily married for twenty-four years.

When you think about it, commercial leasing is a lot like a three- to five-year (or longer) marriage. It's a long-term contract with a lot of expectations on both sides. If you get it wrong, you're in for a lot of fighting, pain, and turmoil. Just like a marriage, if there's a need for a break up, it could cost you a lot of dough.

Tenants and their leases are the key to your income, and that is why, once you come to terms in a Letter of Intent, the second negotiation phase, which requires the actual lease document, is equally as important. In this phase, all the deal points that were agreed upon in the LOI phase are formalized in a legally binding document that regulates how both parties move forward and interact. If you've negotiated well, your tenant is happy and you make a good income.

It's the income your property brings in that will determine its value. That's why leasing is so important, and why I'm devoting a whole book to the subject. Unlike residential real estate, which is valued by market conditions, the commercial real estate investment is valued by two factors: the cash flow it produces each month and the going capitalization rate for the market you're in. Let me explain.

BUILDING VALUE

My first book is almost entirely devoted to talking about valuing a building and building value. Here, I'll provide a brief summary of that discussion. This should in no way be your only education on this complex matter, and if you want to learn more, I encourage you to read my first book, as well as take some courses on property valuation.

The basic equation for determining value in a building is simply:

$$\frac{\text{Net Operating Income}}{\text{Capitalization Rate}} = \text{Value}$$

Following is a sample operating expense spreadsheet and sample pro forma. This will show you a real-life example of determining the value of a 188,000 square-foot office building.

Building Size (SF):	188,025	
OPERATING EXPENSES	2014 Budget Amount	2014 $/SF
Insurance - General	$27,167	$0.14
Electricity and Water	$324,242	$1.72
Building Security Services	$111,327	$0.59
Internal Maintenance Charges	$16,000	$0.09
Operating Supplies - Building Maintenance	$45,000	$0.24
Maintenance & Repairs - Building - Outside Vendors	$35,000	$0.19
Maintenance & Repairs - Building - Contract Work	$250,000	$1.33
Management Fees	$127,194	$0.68
Real Property Taxes	$663,321	$3.53
Occupancy and Building - Subtotal	**$1,599,251**	**$8.51**
Outside Legal Consulting	$692	$0.00
Finance/Audit Fees	$18,416	$0.10
Other Provider Services Fees	$6,167	$0.03
Professional and Outside Services	$25,275	$0.13
Dues	$18,000	$0.10
Rental - Equipment	$150	$0.00
Operating Supplies	$2,000	$0.01
Telephone		$0.00
Supplies and Equipment	$20,150	$0.11
Business Meeting Expense - Meals and Entertainment		$0.00
Travel and Training		$0.00
Operating Expenses	**$1,690,101**	**$8.99**

SAMPLE PRO FORMA		
Building Size (SF)	188,025	
Square Footage Currently Leased	155,070 (82%)	($23.44/SF)
Average Gross Rent(SF/YR) (includes parking)	$3,634,840	($19.33/SF)
2014 Operating Expenses	$1,690,101	($8.99/SF)
NOI	$1,944,739	($10.34/SF)
Market Capitalization Rate	6.5%	
Estimated Value	$29,919,062	($159.12/SF)

NOW FOR SOME QUICK DEFINITIONS

Net Operating Income (NOI): This is the income after operating expenses.

Capitalization Rate (Cap Rate): This rate is determined by the market and is derived by calculating similar properties' net operating incomes divided by their selling price. Determining cap rates seems very simple from the outside but really is a learned art.

So, by way of example, if you had a building with a net operating income of $100,000 in a market with a cap rate of 7 percent, the building's value would be just over $1.4 million.

Now here's where this becomes important. Imagine your lease that provided $100,000 in income expired and you had to take on a new tenant. While you were able to retain the same lease, you made some concessions and mistakes in the negotiation phase, driving up your operating costs, which sent your NOI tumbling down to $90,000. Given the same cap rate of 7 percent, that would mean your building was now effectively worth just under $1.3 million. That's a $100,000 loss in value—not to mention $7,500 a month less in cash flow—all because negotiations on the lease went the tenant's way instead of yours. Ouch. The worst part is you'll be stuck with that loss for years as you wait for the lease to expire.

The good news is you don't have to take a bath on your property. In fact, if you know what you're doing, you can not only increase the value of your property, but you can also determine what you need from a tenant and position your building to find the tenant—and the income—you need to make your investment worth it.

That's what we'll begin to cover in Chapter 2.

CHAPTER 2

POSITIONING YOUR BUILDING

In the 1990s, two-story retail/office buildings were popular in my hometown of Phoenix, Arizona. These buildings had retail space on the bottom and office space on the second floor.

The developer's thinking was that if it was a good idea to build 20,000 square feet of retail space, then it would be a great idea to build 40,000 square feet of leasable space by building office suites on the top floor. Office tenants, it was thought, would like the retail amenities and benefit from the flow of people to the businesses below. In the end, however, this type of building turned out to be a bad idea.

I knew buildings of this type would have a short shelf life and be difficult to rent, even in great locations, and this proved true. For instance, in Tempe, Arizona, the home of Arizona State University— one of the largest universities in the world—one of these buildings sits on a prime real estate corner right across from the East side of the campus, where the baseball and football fields and the basketball arena are located. The location is close to the freeway, thousands of cars drive by each week, and thousands of students live and learn a short walk away. The casual observer would think this would be a perfect property.

The property never really took off, and has struggled since the day it was built. A number of good-sized and reputable restaurants have occupied the bottom floor, but they've come and gone. The worst-performing part of the building is the upper units. Most of them are vacant, making the property a poor performer when it comes to occupancy.

Why would such a seemingly great location perform so poorly? The answer is the design of the building.

Retail users want anchors, big stores like Target or Walmart, next to their space to help draw customers with a retail mindset. Conversely, office tenants want other office tenants with a shared lobby where customers can wait. Most of the time, the user types don't mix well, and only in very high-end, mixed-use developments does it work at all. The two-story office and retail combo buildings lacked what these tenants looked for the most, and, in the process, pleased no one while trying to please everyone—always a recipe for disaster.

Also, some of these buildings were built without elevators, which was a problem for two reasons. One, they weren't accessible for people with disabilities, making them obsolete for modern American Disabilities Act (ADA) regulations. Two, you'd be surprised, but people don't want to walk up stairs to their office. Because of this, the upstairs office spaces were in much lower demand than the lower retail spaces.

The result was much lower leasing rates between the two floors. The bottom floor might lease for $20 per square foot, but the top floor would only command $10 per square foot—which just barely covered the operating expenses. That's a big deal and a lot of lost income. Even worse than the lost income is the type of tenants that elected to rent office space at $10 per square foot—generally not the types of businesses that provide a good customer base for the lower retail space that went for a considerably much higher lease rate per square foot. The result was a strange marriage of fairly reputable retail businesses and lower-grade office businesses.

I guarantee you that some developer bought into that project thinking he'd get the same rental rates or close on both floors. He built a pro forma from those projections, sold investors on it, and took out loans on it. When the income didn't come in and the vacancies stayed steady, it was bad news for that developer.

Financially, going back to our concept of cap rates and NOI, on a 20,000-square-foot building, a $10/SF difference on half a building is $100,000 in lost rental income each year. Based on a 7-percent cap rate, that comes out to more than $1.428 million in lost value—and that's not even counting the costs of high vacancy and carrying operating costs.

KNOW YOUR BUILDING

The point of all this is, the first key to successful leasing is to know your building inside and out. For the keen investor, there should be no surprises when it comes time to lease your property. You should be familiar with every aspect of the property, including its strengths and weaknesses, and, based on those factors, you should be ready to position your building to the right type of tenant in the best possible way.

The investors and developers who get into the most trouble are those who don't have the experience and know-how needed to understand a building's potential pitfalls. That's what happened with the building across from ASU. It was a great location with a great demographic, but it was the wrong kind of building for the area and the clientele. In the end, the weaknesses of that building couldn't be overcome, and it's struggled since the day it was built.

CHAPTER 2

TYPES OF COMMERCIAL REAL ESTATE

Before we move on, I'm going to take a quick moment to define the various types and classes of commercial real estate and examine the strengths and weaknesses of each.

Retail: Every American is familiar with retail. Shopping is our national pastime. Retail commercial space includes shopping centers, strip malls, big-box malls, and mom-and-pop shops.

Pros: Retail is the most scientific of all commercial demographics. Access and visibility drive tenants and value. Strong retail tenants know their customers and they can match their locations with area demographics to give themselves the best chance for success. Other specialties do not have this capability.

Cons: Retail is fickle and joined at the hip with the economy. When the economy takes a dive, retailers can go out of business quickly and a solid lease can become worthless in a matter of months. Also, the grass is always greener in retail. Once-hot shopping malls now fight for meager retail clients as better-located, newer, and higher-quality shopping centers have emerged. Retail trends change over time, as well, and that changes an owner's preferred design and needs from a retail site. Many buildings simply become obsolete because of preference, despite the fact that they are functionally sound.

Office: When most people think of commercial real estate, they think of office space. Office buildings and condos are plentiful. You see them everywhere you go. Every company needs an office and most of us go to our second home every day from 9 to 5...or 6...or 7. Office buildings come in all shapes and sizes, from small, stand-alone buildings to skyscrapers.

Pros: Because office is so diverse, most investors, whether first-timers or seasoned veterans, can find a deal that fits their investment criteria. This gives an easy entry and allows for the ability to build a steady portfolio and move up into bigger deals.

26

Cons: Office space can quickly outpace demand, making for greater vacancy and lower rental rates. The office market is very cyclical, and investors should pay close attention to the state of the market. Leasing this type of property is the most difficult, as tenants' wants are the driver, not any set of objective criteria. Tenants don't always pay extra for higher quality either.

Industrial: Industrial buildings range from small, mixed-use spaces in the low thousands of square feet, to giant warehouses hundreds of thousands of square feet in size, to super-industrial properties that now have more than 1,000,000 square feet under the roof of a single building. A variety of tenants—from research to manufacturing—utilize industrial space.

Pros: Like office, industrial space comes in so many different shapes and sizes that it works well for just about any type of investor. Users typically require less tenant improvement dollars.

Cons: Just like office space, industrial space can be quickly overbuilt, leading to high vacancy and lower rents.

Health Care: Most people think of hospitals when healthcare real estate is mentioned, but the field is much more diverse and includes nursing homes, medical condos, and assisted-living facilities.

Pros: People always need healthcare. Therefore, recessions and downturns don't affect these spaces and businesses as much as others. Additionally, there is a diverse range of business types in the medical industry to match various investor profiles, and medical tenants tend to avoid moving, which means many become good, long-term tenants.

Cons: The medical profession is always in a state of flux, especially with stricter government regulation and insurance reform. Therefore, while the industry overall is strong, there are different types of businesses within the medical industry whose fortunes rise and fall with the times. It's important to have the right mix of tenants in your buildings.

Self-Storage: You've probably seen these around town and maybe even use one. They're the small-unit facilities where people and businesses store anything from extra furniture to archived files. They also tend to rent out trucks and moving equipment.

Pros: Self-storage is pretty much recession-proof and management is relatively easy.

Cons: The barrier to entry is very low for self-storage, and it's easy for competitors to sweep in and undercut your pricing. This erodes margins and lowers property values.

Hospitality: Hospitality is comprised of hotels, motels, casinos, bed-and-breakfasts, resorts, and more. These range in size from small, mom-and-pop businesses to large, multibillion-dollar complexes and mega-sized theme parks.

Pros: When the economy is hot, people spend freely and go on vacation. Additionally, people love to spend money when vacationing and are willing to pay more than they would for usual items like food, drinks, and trinkets. This makes for high margins.

Cons: Hospitality lives and dies with the economy. During downturns and recessions, the industry struggles mightily.

This is obviously a general overview of all product types and their main features. There are many factors affecting every type of commercial real estate, including: location, access, functionality, technological changes, and others. For a more detailed review of this, please refer to my book *How To Win In Commercial Real Estate Investing.*

CLASSIFICATIONS

Within each asset class, there are also varying degrees of property quality that will attract different types of tenants and require different types of marketing to lease well.

It's important to understand asset classifications and where your property is on the scale in order to lease your building well and maximize your profits.

Class A: Class A properties are generally newer and higher quality. These properties are in good locations, utilize modern design techniques, boast high-quality finishes, and are wired for the latest technology.

They're the Rolls Royces of the commercial real estate world, and they're priced accordingly. Usually, because the prices are so steep and returns so modest, class A properties are owned by big funds looking for a steady return. Many institutional investors treat class A buildings like annuities.

Class B: Class B properties are middle-class-type properties in good to decent locations. They are in good condition, highly rentable, and solid properties. Though they rent for less than class A properties, they are easier to find and often present opportunities for improvements that may add value.

Class C: Class C properties are usually older in nature—and they show it. Class C properties often have some sort of "functional obsolescence" such as poor parking or limited technology capabilities. Also, they tend to be in less-than-desirable areas of town.

While understanding the types of buildings available and the classes they fall into is important, the most important thing is to know your building inside and out. When it comes to marketing your building for leasing, there should be no surprises.

KNOWING YOUR BUILDING

Have you ever sat down to fill out a form only to realize you don't have all the information you need? When you tried to hunt down the information, did you have to look in multiple places, spending much more time to do a simple task than you'd ever imagined? I think we've all been there before, and it's frustrating.

In my years as a professional in commercial real estate, I've been amazed at the number of owners who don't know even the simplest details of their properties. When we've asked for it, it's taken much longer than you'd have expected to track it all down.

In this section, I'm going to run you through some simple forms you should fill out to keep your building's information in one spot. Gathering this information beforehand and having it stored in an easy-to-find and central location will save you frustration down the road.

The Building Information Form

The first thing you should do is compile your building's basic data. Use a simple information form for this that has pertinent details such as square footage, building class, number of units, number of floors, the amenities, common areas, zoning, utilities, and more. Here's a sample form.

Building Information Form	LEE & ASSOCIATES COMMERCIAL REAL ESTATE SERVICES
1. BUILDING	
1.1 GENERAL INFORMATION	
Bldg. Name	
Bldg. Address	
Bldg. Age / Year Built	
Number of floors	
Total RSF	
Available Rentable Square Feet	
Total Net Usable Square Feet	
Building is within safe walking distance of restaurants and community services (yes/no)	
Building is within close walking distance of public transport	
1.2 SITE	
Total area of site	
Site subject to flooding?	
100 year flood plain	
Distance to Airport	
1.3 PARKING	
Available spaces/1,000 RSF	
# of available spaces	
# of total spaces	
Age of Parking Lot	
Parking Lot Lighting (foot candles)	
Traffic Counts	
Covered	
Open	
1.4 PUBLIC TRANSPORTATION	
1.5 BUILDING AMENITIES	
1.6 HANDICAPPED ACCESSIBILITY	
1.7 LAVATORIES	
2. BASE BUILDING – STRUCTURE	
2.1 STRUCTURE	
Type of Construction	
Size of floors	
Rentable	
Net Usable	
Finished ceiling height	
Column spacing	
2.2 ROOF- Type/Age	
2.3 BUILDING ENVELOPE/WINDOWS	
2.4 BUILDING INTERIOR	
Ceiling Type (Plenum/Non-plenum/Any asbestos history)	
Is core drilling of the floor slab allowed and are there any limitations?	
3. VERTICAL TRANSPORTATION	
3.1 PASSENGER ELEVATORS	
No. of passenger cabs	
Freight Elevators - Number, Capacity	

CHAPTER 2

Building Information Form	
4. HVAC	
4.1 General Information	
Number of units	
Hours of operation	
After hours cost	
4.2 BASE BUILDING DESIGN CRITERIA AND CAPACITIES	
A. Type of air system constant or variable volume	
B. Air System Operating Parameters	
4.3 BASE SYSTEM DESCRIPTION	
A. Type of System	
B. Distribution of Outside Air	
C. Ashrae Compliance	
5. POWER / TENANT ELECTRICAL DESIGN CRITERIA	
5.1 POWER DISTRIBUTION	
A. General	
Total base building electrical service (Volts/Amps/KVA)	
B. Character of building service to the floor (identify)	
C. Riser configuration	
D. Service entrances	
E. Tenant usable power	
F. Access to additional power	
G. Power/data distribution on floor	
5.2 GROUNDING	
Describe the grounding configuration	
5.3 GENERATOR- Size, Fuel Type, Capacity	
5.4 ELECTRICAL - ADDITIONAL COMMENTS	
6. TELECOMMUNICATIONS	
6.1 TELECOM SERVICES - Cable, Satellite, Internet	
6.2 TELECO SERVICE ENTRY / VAULTS	
6.3 TELECOMMUNICATIONS RISER - Available Space	
6.4 IDF CLOSETS SPECIFICS	
6.5 TENANT TELECOMMUNICATIONS EQUIPMENT	
Available roof space for tenant equipment? How much?	
7. FIRE & LIFE SAFETY	
7.1 SPRINKLER SYSTEM - Fully Sprinklered? Type?	
7.2 FIRE/SMOKE ALARM SYSTEM	
Fire/Smoke alarm system	
Class-E Fire Alarm System (Y/N)	
7.3 ELEVATOR FIRE RECALL	
Explain procedures	
7.4 GENERAL FIRE & LIFE SAFETY	
8. SECURITY	
8.1 SECURITY STAFFING	
Security Personnel – building or contract	
8.2 ACCESS INTO BUILDING / SECURITY SYSTEM	
8.3 LOBBY SECURITY	
8.4 PARKING SECURITY	
9. FINANCIALS	
Operating Expense History	
CAM Charges	
Insurance Costs	
Real Estate Taxes	
Property Tax History	
Association Dues	
10. OTHER	
10.1 MISCELLANEOUS	

Lee & Associates
COMMERCIAL REAL ESTATE SERVICES

The Neighborhood Drive-by Guide

Another good form to have on hand is a simple worksheet that assesses the condition of your building's neighborhood. The worksheet we use at my company, Lee & Associates, establishes the geographical borders of the neighborhood and assesses things like the condition of buildings and cars in the area, the types of businesses, traffic patterns, landscaping, and more. We use a simple scale consisting of the numbers 1 through 5, with 1 being poor and 5 being very good.

Additionally, we put some thought into where the neighborhood will be in five years and ten years. Basically, we're asking if the neighborhood is on its way up or on its way down.

Drive Guide — The Neighborhood Environment

Below are the things you need to look for as you drive neighborhoods and look at environments. (Rating scale: 1 is poor, 2 is fair, 3 is average, 4 is good, 5 is very good) Add comments to right.

Neighborhood Environment: _____ *(list area)*

Border: N_____ / S_____ / E_____ / W_____

						(Comments)
Overall upkeep	1	2	3	4	5	_____
General condition of buildings	1	2	3	4	5	_____
Quality/condition of cars in area	1	2	3	4	5	_____
Quality of businesses in area	1	2	3	4	5	_____
Traffic patterns	1	2	3	4	5	_____
Area landscape	1	2	3	4	5	_____
Overall visual interest	1	2	3	4	5	_____
Perceived prestige	1	2	3	4	5	_____

Would I buy here? Yes No If yes, what product type? _____

On what street(s) would I own? _____

Your Feelings and Impressions:

High points?	Morning	Noon	Night
	_____	_____	_____

Low points?	Morning	Noon	Night
	_____	_____	_____

Future outlook?

In 5 years _____

In 10 years _____

Other Impressions: _____

Questions I need answered: _____

Intuitively, you already know why assessing a building's neighborhood is important. As a homeowner or renter, you know how important location is. Most people spend some time checking out a neighborhood they're going to live in before they even decide to rent or own a home, no matter how nice that home is.

If you're an upper-middle-class parent and spouse looking at a home in a neighborhood that has unkempt yards with cars on blocks, is close to a crime-ridden strip mall, is close to the local college, and is full of college students who throw parties late into the night, you're going to think twice about moving your family into that area no matter how nice the property is. Why? Because you have different needs from those of college students—like safety, peace, and quiet.

Conversely, if you're a single, poor, college student, a property like that might be just the kind of place you're looking for because it's close to the college, cheap, and there are a lot of people in the neighborhood just like you. It meets your needs for the present time.

Businesses are no different. Each business will have needs that your property should meet in order to be a good fit. Your job as a landlord is to know your building well enough to position it as meeting the needs of the potential tenant better than any other building on the market. That takes an honest assessment of the neighborhood and the building, which brings us to the third form to have on hand: the Building Drive-by Guide.

The Building Drive-by Guide

The Building Drive-by Guide is another simple form with a number system for value of 1 through 5. This one is less about the architectural, technical details of your building and, instead, records the general impressions of the building itself. I'm talking about things like curb appeal, physical condition, parking, existing tenant base, landscaping, and more.

Drive Guide — The Building

Below are the things you need to look for as you drive and look at buildings. You'll want one form for each building you view. (Rating scale: 1 is poor, 2 is fair, 3 is average, 4 is good, 5 is very good)

Building Name: _____

Building Address: _____

						(Comments)
Location within area	1	2	3	4	5	_____
Curb appeal	1	2	3	4	5	_____
General condition	1	2	3	4	5	_____
Parking	1	2	3	4	5	_____
Lighting	1	2	3	4	5	_____
Access/entrance and exit	1	2	3	4	5	_____
Tenants	1	2	3	4	5	_____
Ease of finding	1	2	3	4	5	_____
Landscaping	1	2	3	4	5	_____
Fits with your needs/wants	1	2	3	4	5	_____

Your Feelings and Impressions:

High points?	Morning	Noon	Night
	_____	_____	_____

Low points?	Morning	Noon	Night
	_____	_____	_____

Future outlook?

In 5 years _____

In 10 years _____

Additionally, just like with the neighborhood form, you'll ask where the building will be in five years and ten years. Again, you're trying to determine if the building is on the way down or on the way up.

AN HONEST ASSESSMENT

At the end of the day, the point of all this legwork is to make an honest assessment of your investment and how to best position it in the market, because, as we'll talk about in the next chapter, one of the most important components of leasing is marketing. In marketing, the more information you have, the better your ability to get what you want—or at least have realistic expectations.

So, during the process of getting to know your building and its surrounding community, you must understand the strengths and weaknesses of the building.

For instance, if you are looking at a building with limited parking, that's a weakness. Many potential tenants don't want anything to do with buildings that have parking issues. Understanding that your building has parking issues, however, will better equip you to overcome objections that potential tenants might have. Understanding your building's strengths, like environmental upgrades that keep utility costs low, can be used to counteract weaknesses and entice a quality tenant despite weaknesses.

At the very least, understanding your building's weaknesses can help you narrow down your marketing efforts and identify potential quality tenants more easily.

When you understand the strengths, weaknesses, and what makes your building unique, you're in that much better of a position to maximize its potential, and you're ready to begin marketing. We'll cover that in the next chapter.

CHAPTER 3

LEASING IS MARKETING

Every day on my drive to work, I pass many buildings with signs in front of them that read, "For Lease." Some of these signs have been posted for a long time. Each one of them is an attempt at marketing a building—and a reminder of lost income as the properties sit vacant.

I feel for investors who have buildings sitting empty for a long time. There's nothing more painful than paying the bills each month with no income coming in.

When I see a sign sitting in front of the same building for months and months—and sometimes even years—I wonder what the owner is doing. I especially wonder when it's the same sign with the same brokerage listed. What are the steps the broker and owner are taking to market the building? Are they actively seeking out potential tenants, working ceaselessly to track down leads, and exploring every angle? Or are they content to sit there and let the sign do all the work, hoping the occasional passerby will call to inquire about the building? I hope it's the former, but I have to believe that nine times out of ten it's the latter.

It's a shame that many people think successful marketing means putting a sign in front and sending out a hope and a prayer. Many fortunes have been lost and many deals ruined by a fundamental misunderstanding of the effort and work it takes to market and lease a building.

As we've touched on earlier in the book, the key to successful leasing is positioning your building and finding the perfect match. That doesn't happen passively. Even if you put a sign out front and get some phone calls, most of the time you won't have what the caller is looking for. That's because a sign gives little to no details. So you end up wasting both your time and the prospect's time—and, as they say, time is money.

The key to successful leasing is to understand that leasing is marketing. Marketing is hard work that takes thoughtful planning. In this chapter, you'll learn how to put together a winning marketing plan for your property that will greatly increase your chances of leasing your building in a reasonable amount of time, finding the perfect tenant, and maximizing your income.

THE MARKETING PLAN

The marketing plan is your playbook for getting your building leased and leased well. Like any good playbook, it will have some great offensive strategies for getting your building out into the market and securing great tenants, and it will also have defensive strategies for making sure you find the right fit for your property and for answering any objections potential tenants might have.

At my company, my brokers put together a comprehensive marketing strategy for every client's property. We've refined this process over many years and bring to the table decades of experience that has helped us become one of the largest commercial brokerage companies in the nation.

Through those years of experience, we've learned there is no such thing as a cookie-cutter approach to marketing—at least not if you want to be successful. That being said, every marketing plan should have the same general components. The art of leasing happens in adapting those components to the individual properties you're leasing in order to best position that asset in the market.

In this chapter, I'll share with you the components we use at Lee & Associates to successfully build winning marketing plans for our clients. This is invaluable information that my team has developed over many years. I'm happy to share it with you, but I also encourage you to think like an artist, tailoring this information to your particular situation and portfolio. By doing so, you'll be more successful than you could imagine.

A successful marketing plan will have four components: a determination of your property's strengths and weaknesses, a plan for engaging the market, a timeline for executing the plan, and a market analysis.

DETERMINE STRENGTHS AND WEAKNESSES

As we talked about in the last chapter, prior to preparing your marketing plan you need to determine the strengths and weaknesses of your building. I gave you some helpful advice and forms in order to help you accomplish that.

After a full analysis of your building and its surrounding neighborhood, you'll have a good understanding of the things you'll need to highlight in your marketing plan, as well as the potential objections prospective tenants might have and the challenges you might face in trying to lease your building.

For instance, my team was hired to lease a building in North Central Phoenix, which is an office corridor with a number of high-rise buildings and high-end businesses. The building itself was older but in good shape and constructed well. It was owned and partially occupied by a national title company. This fact, as well as the good condition of the amenities, made it ideal to market to higher-end tenants such as marketing firms, engineering and architecture firms, law firms, insurance companies, and more.

After our initial analysis of the building and its surrounding neighborhood, we came up with the following list of strengths and weaknesses, some of which were related to the building and others which were related to the market.

Strengths

- Quality of development.
- On-site property management.
- On-site bank ATM with access to two full-service retail branches within walking distance.
- Ample parking ratio.
- Central Avenue address.
- Light Rail access.
- Located at a high-traffic intersection.

Weaknesses

- Very competitive market due to the amount of available space.
- Floor plans oddly shaped.
- Building considered dated.
- Prestige of existing rent roll—very few well-respected tenants.
- Ceiling grid and restroom conditions poor in select areas.

It's important to note that every building has weaknesses. In this case, it would be easy to have rose-colored glasses and focus on the great location. The reality is, despite being a solid asset, the building still had its challenges, both external and internal.

We knew there would be challenges in attracting a higher-end tenant due to the age of the building and the existing tenant base. As such, we knew we needed to focus on the building's strengths, which included the location of the building, the quality of the construction (which would counteract its age), the great parking, and the access to the newly-built light rail system. It was our belief that these pluses would outweigh the minuses, but it was important that we identified the minuses so the tenant wouldn't surprise us in the middle of a tour or while negotiating the Letter of Intent.

Also, our analysis of the property's strengths and weaknesses allowed us to assess the building's capital needs based on the surrounding market and the building's condition. We then made recommendations to the client that we felt would better position the building in the market and increase the chances of finding a better tenant. Our recommendations were, at minimum, to create move-in-ready spec suites in order to more effectively show the building to potential tenants and to patch up the painting and parking garage. We also gave additional recommendations that we felt were optional but would increase the property's competitive advantage. These were to refurbish the restrooms and elevators, repair an uneven ceiling grid, replace wall coverings on one of the floors, and consider building out the entire fourth floor.

At the end of the day, it's important to be aware of the cost versus benefits of these types of improvements. This requires an understanding of the market and current construction costs. There are always improvements that can be done that will be reasonable in cost for the return gained in higher rents and better tenants. Like most things, this is an art and takes time to learn.

ENGAGING THE MARKET

As I wrote at the beginning of this chapter, many people's idea of engaging the market is to put up a sign, say a prayer, and sit by the phone. That's not very effective—and it's also lazy. A successful marketing plan will map out a variety of ways in which you plan to engage the market. Generally, the market breaks down into two parts:

business-to-consumer (B2C) and business-to-business (B2B). And if you or your brokerage team is going to market your property well, both areas need to be engaged.

Business-to-Consumer: In business-to-consumer marketing, you employ techniques that engage potential tenants directly. The goal is to have a conversation with a company's decision makers, pitch your property, and hope you can lure them from their current offices to yours. This requires a lot of "shoe leather," hitting the streets and making calls. You can't be shy or afraid of rejection, and you need to know what you're talking about. It also takes time, and generally, a lot of it. You can't do this once and wait for your building to fill. Rather, consistency is imperative here. You need to work the phones and meet with potential clients day in and day out. The following are some examples of B2C marketing:

Tenant Rosters: If you have access to tenant rosters, it's very beneficial to take a look at existing ones for other buildings in the area. If not, go get the roster by seeing what tenants are in your competition's building—and call or canvass to find out about upcoming and expiring leases. You can then contact these tenants directly to see if they are looking for a new space or are willing to consider moving. This is where it's helpful to have a broker, as they have access to this type of material. For instance, my firm has a database with many tenants in the market and their lease terms.

High-Level Cold Calls: It's helpful to build a huge database of high-level decision makers at businesses. Part of your B2C marketing strategy needs to include cold-calling decision makers to pitch them on the property. A note: Be ready for rejection and don't give up. Cold calling is not fun at the beginning, especially because many people don't like to sell. But it's essential for success.

Scouting Businesses Tied to Existing Clients: There's a good chance that many businesses are tied both to existing clients for your firm and to tenants in your building. You can contact these businesses regarding available space in your building.

Listings: There are some listing services that are open to both tenants and brokers. Often, people looking for commercial space will utilize these listing services to find properties that work for their needs. Examples of these listing services are CoStar.com and LoopNet.com.

Brochures: A traditional way to market your property is to build a database of businesses suited for your property type and to create and mail or email a brochure to market your property. These brochures are usually higher quality, have pictures of the property, provide property details and market information, and serve as sales pieces.

Spec-Suite Program: Many times, when people want to rent an apartment or purchase a house, they tour spec units that are fully finished and furnished. Seeing the finished product helps people imagine themselves in the space better than seeing an empty space. The same concept also translates well to commercial space. Building out some spec spaces in your property can help you seal the deal during tours.

Signage: While never a sound strategy in and of itself, it's important to not neglect making sure a sign is in front of your building and on the vacant suite doors.

Business-to-Business: Business-to-business marketing involves leveraging the professional networks in your field to work together to lease the building. This happens frequently in real estate where you have brokers representing landlords and tenants respectively, working together to meet their clients' needs. The following are some examples of B2B marketing.

Broker Open Houses: Brokers represent a large pool of potential tenants. It's mandatory to put them to work for you and leverage their relationships. One way to do this is to hold an open house at your property and send invitations to brokers to check out the property and bring their clients. You want to do this right. Make sure the building is in tip-top shape, put out some beverages, and provide some good food.

Email Blasts: At Lee & Associates, we have a huge database of brokers that we use to email our listings. As you work with different brokers and brokerages, it would be beneficial to build your own database and use it to send out your listings.

Brochures: Just as you would send brochures to potential tenants, it's helpful to send out those same brochures to the various brokerages on a regular basis so that they can make their clients aware of your property.

Leverage Relationships: As you gain more experience in commercial real estate, you'll find out it's a relatively small world of brokers, owners and decision-makers with many potential tenants. Along the way, you'll make valuable relationships and contacts. Don't be afraid to pick up the phone and leverage these relationships to help get your property leased. You'll be surprised how ready people are to help out—and at the results it will bring.

Professional Listing Services: Listing services like CoStar.com and LoopNet.com also have premium packages to which many brokers and real estate professionals subscribe. It's helpful to utilize these services, knowing that professionals will search them.

BUILDING A TIMELINE

The process of successfully leasing a commercial real estate property can be a lengthy one. Many new owners are surprised to learn that it can take months or even years to land a solid tenant, and then even longer before the tenant moves in, due to agreed-upon improvements and more. For instance, I just finished a large law firm lease that took twenty-six months from first tour to signed lease. This business is not for the faint of heart.

In order to execute any marketing plan well, it's important to plan a comprehensive timeline that maps out how and when you'll use the tools I've listed in this chapter. When we take on a client at Lee & Associates, we provide them with a detailed timeline.

To give you an idea of what a timeline looks like, here's the one we used for the North Central Phoenix building I've used as an example in this chapter:

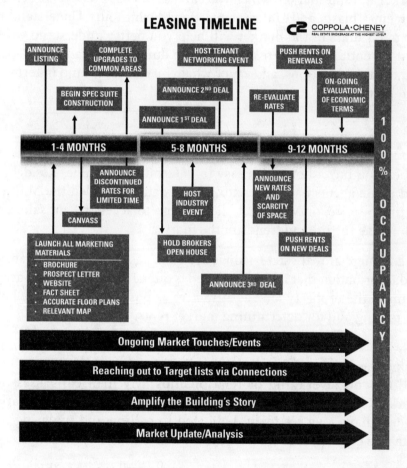

THE MARKET ANALYSIS

Last but not least, it's important to do a full analysis of your property's market and sub-market, which you can use in your property brochure, your email blasts, and to answer questions during tours. Understanding the particulars of the market will help you better understand where your potential tenants are coming from during negotiations, prepare you for any objections, and know what you can command in terms of deal points.

MARKET RENTS

When you buy a house, it's easy to determine the value. Residential real estate agents have access to a large database called the Multiple Listing Service, or MLS, that allows them to access recent sales and determine the pricing trends in the market.

In commercial real estate, things aren't so easy. There's no database, and information that is publicly listed is often inflated or whitewashed to make the property look as attractive as possible. This is true both for pricing and for determining market rents.

Yet, knowing what the going rates and actual comps are for similar properties is essential to leasing well. This takes old-fashioned cold calling and leveraging of relationships. My firm canvasses our markets, talking to both brokers and tenants to determine true market rents. I have a whole team dedicated to calling and updating our database to make sure we have accurate and usable information.

If you don't have the resources necessary to pull together this type of information, I highly recommend you contact and hire a reputable broker and utilize his or her expertise. It will be well worth your time. Later in this book, I'll talk about how to find a good broker.

MARKET CONCESSIONS

Likewise, it's important to understand what types of concessions are in the market. Concessions are simply incentives like free rent, upgraded tenant improvement allowances, termination rights, flexible lease terms, and more.

I just finished negotiating a big law firm deal. Not only did they get free rent, a huge tenant improvement allowance, and a moving allowance; we were able to get totally free parking for the term, signage, free membership to the health club, and even free membership to the private dining club across the street.

It's important to understand the concessions in a market because they affect the bottom line. Even if you collect a higher-than-average market rent each month, too many concessions can eat away your profits and actually make your income effectively less than market.

As with rents, determining market concessions takes rolling up your sleeves, picking up the phone, and talking with brokers and tenants—and you need to know all this information before you start meeting with prospective tenants.

Market Lease Types: As we talked about in Chapter 1, there are a number of different types of leases in commercial real estate. Each market, sub-market, and property type will vary in the market-standard lease type. It pays to know which leases are used in your market.

Market TIs: In each market, a varying amount of money is allocated to tenant improvements. In some markets, landlords might need to agree to pay for all TIs in order to seal a deal. In other markets, they might pay for part and the tenant would pay for part. In still other markets, the tenant pays for all the costs and simply gets the landlord's signoff.

The costs for TIs can be substantial and can significantly impact the bottom line. It's essential to fully understand how they are agreed upon in your market. Not knowing could cost you a lot in potential income when it comes to lease negotiations.

Lease Comparables Report: After you've done the hard work of profiling your property type as described in Chapter 2, you'll be able to identify other properties in your sub-market that match your property's profile. You or your broker can then canvass those buildings and determine their leasing rates and what kind of concessions and TIs they're offering. This is more specific than a general market survey in that it gives you a picture of what properties similar to yours are doing and helps you make sure you're staying at market—or, if you're able, beating it.

DELIVERIES AND CONSTRUCTION

Commercial real estate markets are cyclical. At times, demand is high and it's an owner's market where the owner can command more in rent and offer fewer concessions, if any at all.

In response, developers begin building to meet demand. Eventually, more real estate is built than there is demand for and the market becomes oversaturated. The balance of power shifts to the tenant, who can demand lower rent and more concessions.

It's important to keep an eye on the construction activity in your market. Pay attention to both current construction and planned construction that is in the permitting phase. Additionally, make sure to drill down this information to sub-markets. In many markets, one sub-market may be overbuilt while another part of the city is underbuilt. Don't just look at city-wide statistics and base your marketing and negotiations on that.

Absorption: In conjunction with construction and delivery numbers, you'll want to pay close attention to absorption rates. Absorption is simply the rate at which vacant space is leased. A high absorption rate can indicate that demand is still high while a low absorption rate can indicate that demand is waning. This is the key velocity factor in commercial leasing.

Vacancy: Vacancy is the measurement of how much commercial space is not leased. Tracking vacancy trends gives you a good idea of where the market is heading. Also, beware of thinking a market is healthy just because vacancy is low. Many mature markets have low vacancy but no absorption, so leasing existing vacant space is very difficult. A spike in these measurements can mean a market is on its way to suffering from chronic high vacancy as well. You know what that means—more concessions, lower rental rates, higher cap rates, and a lot of lost money. Below is a sample graph that shows you absorption and vacancy rates.

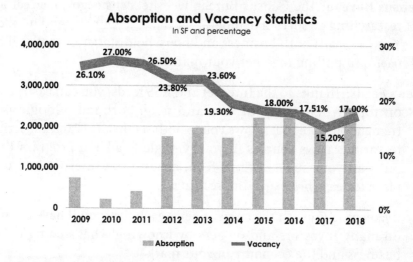

Employment and Employer Information: Commercial real estate is extremely sensitive to economic conditions. Common sense prevails here. If a job market is hot, the commercial real estate market will be as well. If the job market is tanking, there's a good chance the commercial real estate market will be as well.

Pay attention to what kinds of industries and jobs are doing well or suffering. Depending on the type of commercial property you own, you may do well while others suffer, as your property is in demand for a particular business sector. The opposite could be true, too. Knowing what is going on in the job market will help you understand the potential demand for your property. In the end, job creation is the number one figure to track in commercial real estate.

While it's important to do an initial survey of the marketing information I've listed in this section, it's also important to understand that the market is always changing. This type of analysis needs to be updated regularly, and not less often than annually.

Places to Research

If you're planning on pulling this market data together yourself, here's a list of some helpful places from which to pull the information:

Census Bureau: The Census Bureau website, census.gov, is great for researching all sorts of demographic data on your city and market. You can learn both business and household statistics that will be useful in pulling together your market analysis.

News Feeds: Thanks to the Internet and RSS feeds, you can easily stay on top of news in your city and neighborhood. Google is a tremendous tool that allows you to both set up alerts and subscribe to various news sources in your Google Reader, a program that pulls all your subscriptions from around the Internet into one place for easy browsing and reading.

By keeping up with the current news each day, you'll have a jump on many investors and owners by knowing what's going on in business and the economy in your market.

Chambers of Commerce: The local chamber of commerce is great for information on upcoming business deals and business growth, and in connecting you with local business people who can be of help to you. If applicable, join the chamber and be active in local chamber events. At the least, utilize the free resources your chamber offers.

The Urban Land Institute: The Urban Land Institute, found at uli.org, is a well-respected commercial real estate think tank that provides high-quality research on major markets in the U.S. Its materials are very useful. Additionally, it has local chapters in major cities that provide a venue for both local education on real estate market trends and networking with other real estate professionals.

National Association of Industrial and Office Properties (NAIOP): NAIOP represents commercial real estate developers; owners; and investors of office, industrial, retail, and mixed-use properties. It provides information and has seminars and conventions, all just to discuss commercial properties.

The National Retailers Federation (NRF): NRF is a one-stop shop for market data and analysis on the retail sector of commercial real estate and is the largest such organization. It provides national and local education opportunities, networking, conferences, and research, and it publishes a magazine called *Stores*.

Building Owners and Managers Association (BOMA) and the National Property Manager's Association (NPMA): These organizations are made up of the owners and managers of commercial real estate properties. They track industry expenses and changes in laws that affect owners and managers, and provide research and education on all things dealing with commercial property management.

A BROKER CAN HELP

If all of this sounds a little daunting and overwhelming, there's good news. You don't have to do it all by yourself. Having a relationship with a good, reputable broker can be a huge benefit. Most brokerages create these types of market reports on a quarterly basis and some even do well-produced and comprehensive annual reports that are very useful. Most brokerages give this information away for free. Later in the book, I'll give you ten great tips for finding a good broker.

In the end, whether you use a broker or not, having this information at your fingertips will give you a significant advantage when it comes time to show your property and when you're ready to enter the negotiation phases, topics we'll cover over the next two chapters.

CHAPTER 4

LEASING IS SELLING

In the previous chapter, we talked about the importance of building a killer marketing plan, the playbook for getting your building leased and leased well. As any coach knows, it's no good having a great playbook if your team can't execute the plays you've drawn up. So, while leasing is marketing, leasing is also selling, which is the execution of your marketing plan to find the best tenant possible for your building.

A lot of property owners I talk to don't understand the importance of selling when it comes to leasing property. Maybe this is because selling feels more final and a lease doesn't seem to have the permanency of a sale. The reality is, it takes more sales skills to lease a property than it does to sell one—because leasing is very different from buying a property. Selling is black-and-white; if you like the building, the price, and the terms, you buy. Leasing is a two-way relationship between an owner and a tenant that, as I wrote earlier, is much like a marriage. It's far from black-and-white.

The ability to find prospects, meet with potential tenants, show a property well, assess the quality of the business and tenant, cater your pitch to each individual potential tenant, overcome potential objections, minimize shortcomings, and position benefits requires a special skill set that often takes years to develop—if it develops at all.

Client interaction is so important that I don't allow new brokers at my firm to interact with clients until they are a full year into our intensive training program. All it takes is one bad experience for a potential tenant to bail out and for a million-dollar deal to fall through. We don't take leasing lightly, and neither should you.

Selling a prospective tenant on a particular space definitely falls into the art category when it comes to skill sets. As Blair Singer teaches in his book *SalesDogs*, there are many different types of salespeople. It's not so much the style of sale that wins out in the end, but the ability of the salesperson to understand his or her weaknesses and strengths, and to master his or her own style.

Unfortunately, this book—or any book, for that matter—can't make you a good salesperson. That takes hard work, tenacity, study, and years of practice. I can give you some helpful hints to at least get you started on your sales journey, especially when it comes to commercial real estate leasing.

SPACE ALWAYS FOLLOWS THE BUSINESS

When it comes to leasing a building, not just any space will do for a business. Rather, a business will always seek out a space that best reflects what it does, how it does it, its corporate culture, and what will help it succeed.

For instance, a graphic design and marketing firm wouldn't generally seek out a space that was boxy, one-dimensional, and full of cubicles. Instead, that type of business tends to gravitate toward spaces that have character and allow for creativity.

Similarly, a large call center would never look for a space that was immaculately finished, on the top floor of a building, and featuring floor-to-ceiling windows with a view of the ocean. They're not trying to impress anyone. They're just trying to jam as many people into a room as possible to answer phones. Instead, they'll look for a rectangular, utilitarian space suited for cubicles.

For a potential tenant, it's important to be able to envision what a space can be rather than what it is right now. This means if a tenant doesn't think a space is suited for a business simply because they can't imagine what it could be with the right improvements, it's the job of the leasing agent or owner to sell him or her on the vision of what the space can be—to paint a mental picture that is irresistible.

Likewise, if the tenant has a wild imagination but you know the space wouldn't actually be suited for his or her business, you need the fortitude and the knowledge to point that out. You'll save everyone a lot of heartache down the road.

Most owners are so excited about their building that they think everyone else will be as well. They assume if it's good for them or the previous tenant, it's good for anyone. Then they're surprised when potential tenants aren't impressed.

As a side note, let me take this time to point out that when we talk about leasing, sales is a two-way process. Your broker focuses attention on leasing to tenants, but brokers get paid when a lease is done—so they are always selling to the owner, too. That's your fair warning.

You have to be prepared to cast the vision and to do it well. If you can't do that, you won't have a deal and you'll lose a lot of money. Also, don't let your excitement and enthusiasm for your space cause you to blindly accept anyone as a tenant or to not be open to new ideas for the space. Always remember you are in this to make money. You understand your space better than anyone else (or at least you should), and you're best equipped to know who will be a perfect fit or if a new idea will work.

LEASING REQUIRES AWARENESS OF THE RIGHT TYPE OF CLIENT

I've already spoken frequently about the importance of having the right client in a building, so I won't belabor the point here. Part of sales is knowing whether you have the right cat in the bag or not, and being emotionally detached enough to make a good business decision. In sales, the most important thing is not just making a sale but making the right sale. I'll give you an example of what I'm talking about.

There's a building in the Phoenix urban core that has a top-notch location. It's on the corner of a busy street with a lot of retail, walking distance from Arizona State University, close to freeways, in great condition, and next to ample parking. The building struggles to find tenants. Why?

A major bank owns the property and decided to put a call center for the bank in the bottom levels of the building. Call centers are tough tenants and very hard on buildings. Most call centers have six to seven people per 1,000 square feet, and most buildings aren't built for that kind of density. The décor of these spaces is sparse and utilitarian. Toilets are always getting plugged and the interiors are quickly worn. Additionally, call centers are 24/7 and don't pay that much, so they attract a certain type of employee.

When you drive by this building, you'll always see a number of employees out smoking. And when the shifts change, you want to be as far away as possible because employees spill out into the streets in their cars and plug traffic for a good hour.

The decision to put a call center in a building that was in a class A area was a poor one. Higher-end businesses don't want to lease there because they don't want their clients having to deal with the traffic and the haze of cigarette smoke. Higher-end retail businesses and restaurants don't want to lease there because the employees in the building don't make enough to frequent those types of stores and restaurants. The decision to lease to a certain type of business has hampered the potential of a great building for years and affected the entire area. It was the wrong tenant for the building, and it caused long-term consequences.

LEASING IS HARD WORK

It should go without saying that a marketing plan is worthless if it isn't executed well. Executing a marketing plan well is a lot of hard work. Once you've pulled together your market analysis, established rents, planned events, and built your contact database, you must begin prospecting.

At Lee & Associates, this means hundreds of hours on the phone, canvassing (cold calling in person), and meeting with people working in and outside our target location. We have agents making call after call, all day long. Other agents meet with interested prospects to show them the buildings and answer questions. Still other agents pull together the details for broker open houses and field inquiries from other brokerages.

None of these activities is a one-time conversation or event. The selling part of the leasing requires tenacity, diplomacy, and the ability to be extremely detailed. You need to know whom you've talked to, when you've talked to them, and what you talked about. Then you must have a system in place to catalogue all that information and know when to follow up.

At Lee & Associates, we use detailed databases to keep track of this information. This is valuable because the database has all the information from previous interactions in one central place. Below is a sample of spreadsheets we use for canvassing and cold calling.

BUILDING XYZ • CITY, STATE, ZIP CODE   DATE CANVASSED:_____

Suite #	Business Name	Contact Name	Phone #	Square Feet	Lease Expiration	Comments
100	Tenant A	John Smith President	234-6789	2,500	June 1st, 20XX	Dropped off business card and resume
150	Tenant B	Mary Jones Office Manager	321-0987	5,000	Dec 31st, 20XX	Are looking to expand when lease expires
200	Tenant C	Bob Lee CEO	456-7890	3,500	May 31st, 20XX	Set up Meeting to go over market next week

Cold Calling Spreadsheet   Updated as of _____

Tenant	Size	Contact Info	Contact Made (1st Attempt)	2nd Attempt	3rd Attempt	Status	Comment	Results	Commission	# of Hours Required
Prospect 1	3,000	John Smith, 555-9876, CFO	Left voicemail for decision maker	Left second voice-mail		To call 3/12				
Prospect 2	3,500	First Name, Last Name, Phone #, Position	Met with Ed. Has been following my email chains, agreed to use us			Touring on 3/8				

Throughout this process you face rejection after rejection. Yet you need to not only keep going but also keep a clear head to know that even if you do get an interested prospect, it might not be the right fit for your property. You might have to be the one rejecting! Then it's back to the drawing board.

This process can go on for months. You need to have endurance to make it to the finish line. Endurance comes from constant training and practice. I share all this with you not to discourage you but so you know what you're getting into and not lose heart when the going gets tough.

Understanding the process is long, but our service needs to be "Four Seasons" quality. I created a few mandatory items for our team to ensure our clients get the best, most responsive service in the industry. I call it The Velocity of Work. Following is a sample of what that means.

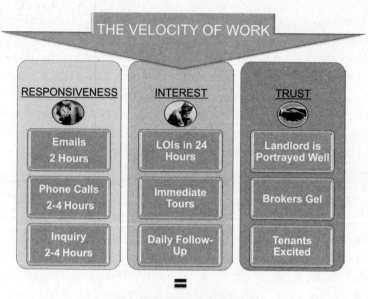

DEAL MAKERS AND BREAKERS

In addition to whether or not a tenant and a space are a good fit, there are a number of other factors that will affect the selling phase. A good salesperson is able to overcome objections, minimize the negative aspects of the property, and amplify the positive ones during the sales phase. Below, I've compiled a partial list of these factors (I'm assuming your building is on a tenant's final "short list" based on location).

Rates: This is the most obvious one. One of the tenant's main concerns will be the rent and the cost per square foot. Every potential tenant will have a budget. It does no good to sell a business on a property they simply can't afford. After all, you want them to pay each month. Conversely, it doesn't do you any good to rent a property well below market simply to get it rented. This is why it's important to understand as best you can both the market and the business to which you're showing the property. Knowledge is power.

Term: When I played professional baseball, I learned something about the time-value of a contract. Many players place as much importance on the term of a contract as they do the pay. This is because the value of a contract can lessen as markets grow. If you make a million dollars for three years, you might be able to make two million dollars in the fourth year, depending on the market and how you've grown as a player. It's not a good deal, then, to make a million dollars a year for five years.

Similarly, in a down market, many tenants may want a longer lease because they want to lock in a low rate for a long time—which will cost you money if the market picks back up. In a hot market, many tenants will try to negotiate a short-term lease in hopes the market will cool and they'll get a better deal down the road. Also, in a tough economy, tenants facing uncertainty may not want a long-term lease if they can't forecast business growth.

At the end of the day, negotiating the term of a lease is just as important as negotiating the rental rates. Many times, potential tenants will want to negotiate the rate based on the term. A good salesperson will know where the market is heading and negotiate accordingly.

Free Rent: Many leases include free rent for a month or more as an incentive to sign on the dotted line. There is an art in giving concessions such as this. A good salesperson needs to be able to know how little they can give in order to get the client to sign. Many inexperienced salespeople are too eager to give away the farm in order to get the lease. They play their hands too quickly. Instead, it's wise to push the deal without concessions and move from there. All this, of course, depends on the market.

Layout: Layout is important for many businesses. As we talked about earlier, a design agency would be looking for an entirely different type of office layout than would a call center. A good salesperson knows the strengths of a property's layouts, the type of clients that would be best suited, and how to sell that client on the space. And that leads to my next item, the cost of tenant improvements.

Tenant Improvements: Most lease agreements have negotiated amounts allotted to the tenant for improving the rented space and getting it ready for the business to move into. These are often referred to as "TIs." Again, it's important to know the market. An inexperienced salesperson can give away too much—or not be flexible enough—and kill a good deal quickly. It's important to note that, today, owners are creating spec suites, which are completely built-out spaces, in order to take this phase off the table.

Quality of Building: Common sense dictates that a higher-end business won't be interested in a building that is shoddy on the outside, or even just Plain Jane for that matter. For the most part, there's a correlation between the quality of the building and the quality of the business that leases the building. Part of your job as a salesperson is to know what types of businesses would be interested in your property based on its quality.

Parking Type, Ratio, and Location: Nothing is worse than having to spend an extra ten minutes trying to find a parking spot. If a building has a deficiency in parking, it would be smart to find tenants that don't have a lot of visitors to their offices. Conversely, if there is ample parking, a good salesperson is able to leverage that in the sales pitch to potential tenants. Additionally, take into account how far the parking structures and spaces are from the building. Tenants aren't big fans of having to park far away from their offices or having their customers do the same. Also, in some cities, parking is a luxury and sparse and can be a big source of revenue. In some markets, you can charge up to $70 per month for each covered, reserved parking stall. Don't overlook this possible revenue generator.

Efficiency: The best buildings are efficient buildings, meaning they use the space well. That being said, each tenant layout is unique, and certain layouts will be more (or less) efficient in a building and for certain types of tenants.

For instance, in the 1980s, building floor-plates were 10,000 to 15,000 square feet, which was perfect for 5,000-square-foot tenants but not so good for 50,000-square-foot tenants that had to take three to five floors just to have enough space to do business. Today, however, the average floor plate is 25,000 to 30,000 square feet, which is better for larger tenants, but now the smaller tenants can get lost.

As a salesperson, your job is to know how efficient your building is and to be ready to make concessions, minimize defects, or highlight strengths to a potential tenant.

Signage: Signage can be a complicated issue because there are many factors involved. For instance, here in Arizona, local municipal signage laws vary. In North Phoenix, where signage laws are more lax, you'll find bigger, easier-to-spot signs for businesses. However, Scottsdale, a highly affluent city, has strict signage laws, and most signs are very small and hard to spot, especially on the faster roads. No matter the municipal laws on signage, tenants will want the best placement and visibility possible when it comes to signage.

Amenities On-Site: Depending on their needs and clientele, some businesses will want buildings that have on-site amenities such as a sundry shop, restaurants, health clubs, copy centers, conference rooms, and more. These types of amenities tend to be in bigger, more expensive properties that attract higher-end businesses.

Amenities Off-Site: The proximity of places to eat, stores, parks, clients, and more can be important to a potential tenant. A good salesperson will pay careful attention to highlighting amenities close to the property, especially if the potential tenant would find that a big selling point.

Property Management: A good property management company keeps the property looking immaculate and promptly takes care of issues that arise—and believe me, issues do arise. This makes property management a big selling point because it offers peace of mind for your tenants.

Ownership: If you own a building, you'd better not be a jerk or financially unstable. Because leasing is like a marriage; it requires two parties who can get along. If you're both the owner and the leasing agent for your property, keep at the top of your mind the fact that your potential tenant is sizing you up just as much as you are sizing up him or her.

Americans with Disabilities Act (ADA) Compliance: For many businesses, it's important that a building is ADA compliant. That means if you have an older building that isn't ADA compliant, you'll be limiting your pool of potential tenants. Adjust your sales pitch accordingly.

Location: Location is (or should be) the most important request for a business. Many types of businesses form clusters. For instance, businesses that use helicopters and airplanes, and businesses that service those types of companies, congregate around airfields and air parks. Medical professionals, and companies that service them, gather close to hospitals. The list goes on and on. Be aware of the businesses that are in your area and use that as a selling point for potential tenants that could benefit from being located in the same vicinity.

EVALUATING PROPOSALS

If you've done your job right, you'll get requests for proposals (RFPs) to lease your property. An RFP details all the terms of a potential lease and some marketing information. Following is a sample proposal.

March 15, 2013
Broker Contact
Address
City, State, Zip

RE: TENANT

Dear Broker:

BROKERAGE NAME has been retained to assist _____ (**"Tenant"**) in the evaluation of its facilities needs. To aid us in our analysis and further discussion, please respond to this Request for Proposal no later than_____ **(Date)**.

The RFP format is designed to inform you of business points important to (**"Tenant"**) Please address each particular issue in your proposal.

1. **SPACE REQUIREMENT**

   Approximately _____ rentable square feet with expansion options. Space shall be measured by using ANSI/BOMA Z65.1 revised June 7, 1996 and shall be field measured. Please provide a CAD file of the space.

   The maximum rentable space/useable space ratio shall be specified.

2. **LEASE COMMENCEMENT**

   _____

3. **INSTALLATION PERIOD**

   Tenant requires, at no charge, prior to Lease commencement, thirty (30) days prior entry for furniture, cabling, relocation, etc. after completion of tenant improvements.

   Tenant improvement construction period to precede this date at no charge to Tenant.

4. **TERM**

   The term of the Lease will be for a period of ( ) years **from the issuance of Certificate of Occupancy for the Tenant Improvements, but no sooner than (Date).**

5. **RENTAL RATE**

   Please indicate the annual lease rate per rentable square foot to be charged over the term. Please specify amount of free rent, if any, as a concession.

6. **TENANT'S SHARE OF OPERATING EXPENSES AND REAL PROPERTY TAXES**

   _____ Base Year grossed up as if the project was 95% leased. This shall include fully assessed real estate taxes.

   Controllable operating expenses shall not be increased more than three percent (3%) per annum, non-cumulative, which shall exclude utilities, real estate property taxes, and insurance premiums.

   Please provide 2011 actuals and 2012, 2013 budgets, expense breakdowns and address your willingness to "lock" your expense estimates.

7. OPTION TO EXPAND

Tenant shall have a hard option to expand between the 60th – 71st month of the lease for not less than 5,000 square feet and not more than 8,000 square feet. Said space shall be contiguous and be previously built to __("Tenant")__ standards, or similar tenant improvement allowance as provided for the initial space..

8. RIGHT OF FIRST REFUSAL

Tenant shall have the "Right of First Refusal" on any contiguous space located on its floor(s). Tenant shall have fifteen (15) working days to respond from receipt of Landlord's written notice with a "Letter of Intent" and thirty (30) working days to space plan and finalize the agreement.

9. EXPANSION SPACE TERMS

In the event Tenant leases any part of the expansion space at any time between the first (1st) and twenty-fourth (24th) months of the lease term, the tenant improvement allowance shall be prorated over the remaining term, the rental rate per square foot for said Expansion Space shall be no more than the Tenant's then current rental rate per square foot and the Lease term for such Expansion Space shall be coterminous with the Lease term for the initial Premises. After twenty-four (24) months the Terms and Rate shall be ninety percent (90%) of prevailing market for unimproved space, but taking into consideration commissions, parking, etc. Tenant Improvement allowance for expansion space shall be computed consistent with Paragraph 13.

10. LOAD FACTOR

Please indicate the building load factor for purposes of calculating usable and rentable square footage.

11. OPTION TO RENEW

Tenant shall be entitled to renew the Lease for two (2) additional terms of five (5) years each by first having given Landlord six (6) months prior written notification. The renewal rates shall be no more than the lesser of last year's lease rate or ninety percent (90%) of the then prevailing rental rate, for unimproved office space, considering all market concessions. Within ten (10) days after Tenant shall have given a Renewal Notice, Landlord shall give Tenant a notice setting forth Landlord's estimate of ninety (90%) percent of the prevailing market rate of base rental for the premises for the renewal term. Should Tenant and Landlord be unable to agree on an acceptable market rate within thirty (30) days after delivery of renewal notice, then an arbitration provision shall be engaged to produce a renewal lease rate.

12. RIGHT TO TERMINATE

Tenant shall have the right to terminate the lease at the end of the seventh (7th) year with nine (9) months prior written notice.

13. TENANT IMPROVEMENT ALLOWANCE

Please provide a per square foot tenant improvement allowance of $_____/RSF. Tenant may use any unused portion of the allowance at its sole discretion. Tenant shall be allowed to competitively bid and manage the improvements on an "open book" basis. There shall be no construction management or supervisory fees. In the event Tenant's improvements are in excess of the allowance, Tenant requires the right to amortize the additional costs on a straight line basis over the term of the Lease.

14. MOVING ALLOWANCE
Please provide an allowance to offset Tenant's relocation expenses.

15. SIGNAGE/CORPORATE IDENTIFICATION
Please indicate all signage available to _____ (or a successor entity name) on the building, monument and at the entrance to its space. Landlord will be responsible for the cost of sign(s) and installation.

16. PARKING
Tenant will require a parking ratio of not less than _____. All parking shall be free of charge, including visitor parking for Tenant's customers and clients. This shall include covered garage reserved for all partners and covered garage unreserved for associates and office administration and vacancies for all staff. Additionally, tenants shall require an allowance of 10,000 hours per year, cumulative, for visitor parking validation.

17. HOURS OF OPERATION
Please indicate the normal hours of operation for the subject property and any charges for off-hour operations.

After-hours HVAC charges not to exceed $10.00 per hour per floor. Landlord to provide 50 hours of after-hours HVAC per month at no charge.

18. SECURITY DEPOSIT
Tenant shall provide current corporate financial statements to support waiver of a security deposit. The firm's partners will not personally guarantee the lease.

19. NON-DISTURBANCE AGREEMENT
Tenant requires a Non-Disturbance and Attornment Agreement from any and all current and future lenders and ground lessors of record, now and in the future.

20. HAZARDOUS MATERIAL
Landlord represents that no part of the Premises or building contains asbestos, asbestos-containing material or other hazardous material ("ACHM"). If ACHM is present, the Landlord, prior to delivery of the Premises to Tenant shall, at its sole cost and expense, remove same.

21. TENANT ROSTER
Please provide a current tenant roster for the building.

22. SECURITY SYSTEM
Please describe the building's current security system. Tenant requires access to the premises on a 24/7 basis.

23. CONFIDENTIAL INFORMATION
Both parties agree that all Tenant information, communications and negotiations are confidential. As such, both parties agree to keep all information, correspondence and negotiations strictly confidential.

24. **<u>BROKERAGE AGREEMENT</u>**

Broker and Brokerage Firm name here _____ will be compensated by Landlord per a separate agreement – 50% upon execution of a new lease agreement and 50% upon commencement of the new term.

25. **<u>RESPONSE DATE</u>**

Please respond by _____ **(DATE)**.

This Request for Proposal is not to be construed in any manner as an obligation on the part of Tenant to enter into a lease with any party electing to respond to it.

If you elect to respond to this Request for Proposal, please understand that neither the undersigned nor Tenant assumes any liability for any costs or expenses that you may incur. All proposals submitted become the property of Tenant, and Tenant reserves the right to, at its sole discretion, accept or reject any proposal for any reason or no reason. All responses shall be considered offers, which shall not be withdrawn for thirty (30) days from the date of receipt by Tenant.

If you have any questions about this request or any other aspect of this requirement, please contact our office. This request for lease proposal is not intended to impose any legally binding obligations upon any party, but rather is meant to set forth certain criteria to serve as a basis for further discussion.

Sincerely,

BROKER
Name
Principal
cc: Contacts

There are many factors that go into determining if you want to lease to a prospect. Factors to consider are:

- The type and financial strength of a business.

- The terms you are negotiating, e.g., length of lease, rental rate, concessions, TIs, etc.

- Prior leasing history.

- Your interpersonal relationship with the owners and/or managers with whom you'll be interacting.

It's important that you define your objectives as an owner before evaluating the prospect. What are you looking for? What's most important to you when it comes to filling your space? What's least important?

As we've discussed, leasing is a series of trade-offs. You may be more comfortable with a particular business as a tenant that's asking for a lower rate but a longer lease term than you would be with a less-proven business that is willing to pay more but for a shorter lease term. At the end of the day, it's a subjective decision that is based entirely on your needs, your gut, and your cash flow.

One thing I suggest, however, is do a background check on any business wanting to lease your space. Two aspects of company history are particularly important:

Company Performance: You want to know how the business has performed in the past and especially how it's performed recently. It's standard to ask for financials in order to assess the financial health of the business. Also, ask for references from other businesses and past landlords if you don't know the tenant.

Functional History: Assess how long the company has been in business. Call the references and ask what type of tenants they were. Just like if you were hiring a new employee, if they've moved around a lot to different locations, ask why. You can learn a lot about what kind of tenant you're in for just by doing a little ground work and not being afraid to ask hard questions.

FIVE TIPS TO MAKE YOU A BETTER SALESPERSON

I want to reiterate that one of the most important functions of leasing is your ability to sell well. If you can't sell, don't try to lease.

That being said, I'm a firm believer that anyone who is willing to sell can develop the skills necessary to do so. If you're ready and willing to sell, here are five tips to help make you a better salesperson:

Understand Your Business: There's a television commercial that I find clever. The scene is a big-box electronics store that obviously is supposed to represent Best Buy. The camera is focused on a young salesman trying to sell the customer a laptop, "The difference between the two...?" the salesman says. He bends over and squints as he reads the two cards that give the information about the computers, looks to the camera, and smiles sheepishly. Then the commercial cuts to information about a website for geeks with real reviews by people who know what they're talking about.

The point is clear; if you don't know your product and your business, you're going to be a terrible salesperson. If you're new to commercial real estate, you're facing a learning curve. You need to be diligent to learn as much as you can as quickly as you can. If you don't know your business, people who do will be able to tell. Part of being a great salesperson is having great knowledge about what you're selling.

Build a Process: How will you track your deals and efficiently follow up on them? How will you find deals? When you find them, how will you make them? What will be your strategy for starting and cultivating relationships? How will you multitask and still be successful? What is your tour path? What are you selling? What are the standard objections and how can you overcome them?

All these questions are answered through your ability to build processes that work well for you. A process is a system that allows you to be your most productive, not letting any detail fall through the cracks, and hitting on all cylinders from a lead to a close. Different things work for different people, and it's essential that

69

you determine what your processes will be. Sales is a lot of work, and you need to be able to hold it all together. Dropping the ball will lead to a lost sale—and a lot of lost money.

Practice Makes Perfect: This is a pretty obvious one, but I'll reiterate a point I've made in this book already: Very few people are natural salespeople. Rather, it takes a lot of practice and a lot of deals to perfect your technique. You will fail. But don't let it get you down. Let failure be your guide to success by learning from your mistakes and growing.

As you do more deals, be conscious of the areas where you need to grow and be ready to learn. Review your negotiations and decide where you could have done better and where you hit the nail on the head. Start trying to figure out the fine line between pushing a deal through and knowing when to concede. Work hard at practicing the art of taking an idea and making it real, using your ability to sell to convince people your way is the right way.

See All Sides of the Transaction: It does you no good to be a selfish, money-grubbing, one-sided salesperson. Leasing involves two parties and your job is to understand the motivations of each side and figure out what is a win-win for everyone. Win-win in leasing is paramount. You are at the beginning of a three- to ten-year relationship. Don't get off on the wrong foot.

In the leasing process, nothing is more valuable than trust, and a potential tenant will be able to intuitively sense if you're concerned with coming to terms that are good for everyone or just out to get the best deal for yourself. Taking the honest and human approach to sales not only results in better deals for everyone, it also creates a long-term trust factor that leads to more deals in the future as people come back to you when they need your services and also recommend your services to others.

Be Humble: Nothing is worse than arrogant salespeople who walk all over their clients and their staff. The first thing you have to understand is that no one can make it alone. Give credit and praise to those who helped you be successful. Understand that you would never succeed without them. Also, don't run ahead at full speed and burn yourself out. Take things in stride and understand leasing is a marathon, not a sprint. Know that you don't know everything and be ready to learn, change, and grow—or die. View everyone you come in contact with as someone who can teach you something, and treat them as valuable because of this. Finally, understand that you will not make every deal, and you will lose clients. That's just the nature of the beast. It hurts when it happens, but it happens to everyone. Don't let it get you down. Instead, assess what went wrong and learn.

If all goes well—if you learn the business, understand your property in and out, put together a killer marketing plan, and execute it well on the sales side—you'll land the best tenant available and be ready to start negotiating the lease. That's where you can make—or lose—a lot of money.

In the next chapter, we'll discuss the process of negotiating a lease and cover the important details of this critical legal document.

CHAPTER 5

NEGOTIATING
THE LEASE POINTS

So far throughout this book we've covered what leasing is and why it's important, how to position your building, how to create a winning marketing plan, and how to execute that plan by selling well. To reiterate, there's a certain element of science to these things, but at the end of the day, great leasing is an art form that requires determined practice—and no one masters an art form out of the gate. That takes years of work and stick-to-it-iveness.

If you're feeling a little overwhelmed by what we've covered so far in the book, that's OK. It's a lot to take in, but I promise that if you take the principles I've taught you so far and couple them with hard work and practice—if you're tenacious about improving your skill set as an owner, marketer, and salesperson—you'll be light years ahead of most other people. Remember that you're in a marathon, not a sprint. Keep your chin up, push through, learn from your mistakes, and you can master the art of commercial real estate leasing.

CHAPTER 5

This chapter is going to contain a lot of details—nuts and bolts, if you will. We'll cover the key deal points of a lease and the implications of negotiations concerning those key points. You may find that you're tempted to skim through the sections or move on entirely. I caution you against that.

Marketing and selling are only half the equation. They get your tenant to the door. Negotiating your lease deal points is the other critical half of the process—and the one that puts money in your pocket or takes it out.

In my years in the industry, I've negotiated more than 2,000 leases, and each one was different. Because there is no standard lease when it comes to commercial real estate, it's important to negotiate the deal points of a lease before actually crafting it. This is commonly done through negotiating a Letter of Intent (LOI) between you and the potential tenant before crafting the legal document that binds both parties to those points. By doing this crucial step, you'll save both you and your tenant a ton of legal fees by knowing the framework of the deal before hiring an attorney to craft your lease.

In actuality, negotiating a lease document is beyond the scope of this book. Please don't use this as the authority for doing that. Rather, use it as a guide for the process and hire a good attorney who specializes in commercial leases when you're ready to craft the lease.

When you begin the negotiation process, it's important to remember that each side has motivations, desires, and important deal-breaking points. The goal of the process is to discuss and agree upon all the deal points and then negotiate a document that is beneficial to everyone.

The lease is the legal and binding document that will define your relationship with your tenant and your tenant's relationship with you for years to come. It's important to get it right.

Generally, the process begins with an interested party sending you a proposal for the lease points. From there, you and the tenant (or, more commonly, you or your broker and the potential tenant's broker) will begin a back-and-forth process of negotiation until both sides have reached an agreement on what will go into the lease document itself. Both parties will sign off on the agreed deal points, and they'll be formally crafted into a LOI that will guide the writing of the lease.

DETERMINE YOUR OBJECTIVES

The first and most important thing to do when heading into negotiations is to define your objectives. Every negotiation involves two or more parties that each have competing—and sometimes complementary—objectives. A successful negotiator understands the importance of compromise. Mastering compromise requires understanding which of your deal points are non-negotiable, which can be altered or changed, and which are least important.

I find it's helpful to write these down. Lease terms, criteria, and parameters are crucial to understand and benchmark against a market and competitors that are ever-changing. Everyone has make-or-break deal points. For instance, if you're cash-strapped as an owner, it may be impossible for you to front a large sum for tenant improvements. If a potential tenant asks for this, it would be a deal-breaker. It's non-negotiable. The key to good negotiations, however, is to compromise by standing firm on your non-negotiable points and bending on things you'd like to have in the deal but don't necessarily need.

In this case, you might say no to TIs but yes to a request for a reduction in the rental rate. If your true need was to get the space filled and there was room in your cash flow projections, go a little lower on the rent. If your potential tenant was flush in cash, they might be willing to accept that deal since they could front the costs for the build-out and make up the cash over time through rental savings.

This is just one example of the seemingly endless ways in which you can come to terms during a lease negotiation. At the end of the day, the most important thing is to understand what breaks the deal and what doesn't—and to be vigilant in sticking to your guns on the deal-breakers and ready to concede on everything else.

DETERMINE YOUR TENANT'S OBJECTIVES

Thomas G. Mitchell, in his book *The Commercial Lease Guidebook*, reminds us that everybody has a hidden agenda when it comes to negotiations. Part of a successful negotiation process is determining not just your deal-breakers but also your potential tenant's deal-breakers.

During the sales phase, pay attention to the words and body language of potential tenants. Do the same thing in the negotiations phase. Many times, people will tip their hand and give you some insight into what is motivating them through body language and off-hand comments.

Once you have a good idea of what will break a deal for a potential tenant, you'll be able to stay away from those points and push that much harder on deal points that won't break the deal.

So, without further ado, let's dig into the lease points. These will be the high-level points that every lease negotiation will cover. Each party will have an agenda on each of these issues.

LEASE TYPE

As we discussed in Chapter 1, there are different types of leases, and their usage depends much on the markets in which you're leasing. The type of lease you use will be instrumental in determining some of the negotiation points I've listed in this chapter.

As a refresher, the four main lease types are the following:

Gross: This is a full-service lease. In a gross lease, the landlord pays all utilities, the upkeep of the building, and maintenance costs, and the tenant pays the owner one check each month. In Gross leases, there is usually an escalation clause that allows the Landlord to recoup costs over a negotiated expense "stop" or over a "Base Year" (actual expenses incurred during the base year). For example, if a tenant is using utilities well above the contractual average (or "stop"/"base year"), the owner will require the tenant to pay for those overages.

Net: While there are some nuances to the term "net," it generally means the tenant pays for portions of the costs associated with the property's utilities, upkeep, and maintenance. So, for example, if you have a Net-utilities lease, the tenant pays for utilities.

Triple Net: This is a popular term and a lease for investors looking for a steady return. In a Triple Net (NNN) lease, the owner is responsible for the structure and capital elements of the property, such as the roof, parking lot, etc. The tenant covers all other expenses required for the operation of the building, including utilities, taxes, utility repairs, maintenance, and more. Generally, you find this type of lease for businesses in retail, such as fast food franchises and drug stores.

Absolute Triple Net: In an Absolute Triple Net lease, the tenant pays for everything. This type of lease results in little work for the landlord, but the landlord also gives up a lot of control of the asset. Like everything, there are trade-offs for this type of lease.

Lease types are part of the deal point negotiating process. As the owner, you'll be in a much better position to determine the lease type, as the market pushes this. In most cases, if your expectations are in line with the market, the tenant won't really have a choice. Any space they pursue will use the same type of lease. Nonetheless, there may be times when it could be advantageous to negotiate a different lease type than the market standard. It all gets back to you and your potential tenant's non-negotiable deal points.

TAXES

As the old saying goes, "In life, two things are certain: death and taxes." The good news is, when it comes to commercial real estate leasing, you may not have to pay the taxes at all! Given the right market conditions and the proper negotiating skills, you can have your tenant pay most—if not all—of your real estate taxes by signing a net-taxes lease.

As an owner, it's especially important to minimize your exposure and liability to taxes. Local, state, and national governments are always looking for new and creative ways to tax people and businesses. While taxes are always a certainty, the type of taxes and the rates you'll be taxed at are not. There's nothing worse than putting together a careful deal that pencils well only to have it ruined by a change in tax policy down the road.

The only way to ensure your sweet deal doesn't turn into a sour one is to pass the cost and burden of taxes to your potential tenant. Of course, your tenant is in the same position as you. So, as with almost everything, the taxes are a negotiation point between the two parties.

For both real estate and any other taxes (in Arizona, for instance, we have rental tax that tenants pay), you'll need to determine which taxes will be paid by the tenant and which will be paid by you. The most common taxes are real estate taxes that come from the assessor's office and any assessments added to the tax bill from city bonds to fund various projects like sewers. These aren't the only taxes, however, that can be assessed to a property. Each situation will vary, and it's important to understand your full tax exposure and negotiate accordingly.

Other types of taxes you may need to negotiate are:

Tenant Personal Property Tax: Some cities charge personal property taxes on the assets your tenant owns apart from the building itself. It's important to make sure your tenant is responsible for these and that the lease has provisions for declaring default if they somehow filter up to you.

Gross Income Tax: Rents are taxable in some states. You'll want to make sure you're aware of your state laws and negotiate provisions in the lease for charging these taxes to the tenants.

Conveyance Taxes: Sometimes the need arises for a tenant to transfer a lease to another party. If this is allowed under the lease, it may be an action that is taxable. Be sure to negotiate who is responsible for those taxes, should they apply.

Rental Tax: Some states and municipalities tax rental properties. You need to make sure these rental tax costs are passed on to the tenant, just as a business passes them on to customers purchasing a product. It goes on the monthly rental invoice.

The Proper Pro-Rata Share: If you're negotiating with a tenant to lease a portion of a building in which there are other tenants, you'll need to determine the percentage of taxes the tenant is responsible for within the context of the whole building. This is usually done by calculating the total leasable square footage the tenant will occupy.

The potential tenant will be concerned with making sure the proper calculations are made in determining the leasable square footage. So be ready to provide solid evidence for your determinations and don't be surprised to be questioned on them.

The Right to Contest: Taxes fluctuate each year based on assessments. If your tenant is responsible for these taxes, they'll want the right to contest the assessments. However, because you own the building, the taxes are technically your liability. So it's important to make sure contest rights are granted only after the tenant pays the taxes. Also, contesting an assessment costs money. Make sure to negotiate who is responsible for those costs.

UTILITIES

There are two factors that come into consideration when it comes to utilities: are they adequate, working, and available; and who is going to pay for them? It will be in the best interest of both you and the tenant to work together to make sure all utility hookups and capacity are available and meet the tenant's needs. When it comes to who pays, that will be the subject of another negotiation.

In a net lease, the tenant will be responsible for paying all the utilities; however, the hookup charges will be up for negotiation. In a gross lease, the owner is responsible for the utilities and assesses a portion of the utility costs to the tenant during the base year or up to the stop. In a gross lease situation, you'll want to make sure you have some sort of clause that sets the utility limits. For instance, you wouldn't want a tenant in the middle of a sweltering Phoenix summer to run the air conditioning 24 hours a day at 50 degrees. The cost would be staggering.

You'll also want to discuss a clause for non-liability for interruption. Basically, this gets you off the hook for having to pro-rate the rent to compensate for an interruption in utility service that occurs through no fault of your own.

RENTAL RATES

This one may seem a bit obvious. You want to make as much as possible in rental income and your potential tenant wants to pay as little. There is more to negotiating rent than meets the eye. Besides discussing the rate and deciding on a mutually beneficial deal, there are also other considerations to negotiate surrounding the rent.

For instance, you will want to contractually spell out the day rent is due, where it should be paid (e.g., mailing address, central office, etc.), and what the consequences are for late payment.

Additionally, you'll need to come to terms on when rent payments start contractually. If there are no improvements for the property, this is simple—it's once the tenant signs the contract and/or takes possession of the property. If the tenant needs to do improvements to the space, however, things can get complicated.

Generally, improvements are a somewhat lengthy process. The tenant's architect will usually need to draw up plans, submit them for approval, line up contractors, possibly apply for permits—which can be an extremely lengthy process—and finish the build-out before they can even take possession of the space. More often than not, you will need to negotiate a reasonable amount of time for the tenant to complete this process before requiring them to pay rent. The amount of time will be negotiable, but plan on it being a reality. This means you need to factor the lost potential income into your pro forma projections.

Finally, you'll also need to negotiate concessions. Will you pay a portion of the improvement costs, if there are any? Will you give a month, or two, or three, in free rent? Will you waive certain fees for moving in or cover certain costs associated with move in? All of these questions and more will be deal points that you'll be able to leverage more or less, depending on the market conditions and the sophistication of your tenant. If you're not ready to negotiate well, you can lose a lot of money. Do your homework.

LEASE TERM

Lease term (the time frame of the lease) is a wholly market-related item. At first blush, you might be inclined to think the longer the better. If it's a renter's market, you'll want to consider negotiating a shorter lease to take advantage of a better market down the road. In these conditions, your tenant—if he or she is smart—will want a longer lease to lock in low rents. Conversely, if the market is hot for owners, you'll want a long lease to lock in profits for as long as possible, and your tenant will want to negotiate a shorter lease. Other factors come into play, such as the viability of the tenant's business in the long run or the future expansion plans of that business. Admittedly, it's a bit of a gamble, but a calculated one.

The following are a few other things you'll negotiate besides the beginning and end date of the lease in the lease term phase:

Early Occupancy: Sometimes, your tenant will need to occupy the building to do improvements, move in furniture, set up phones and Internet, and more before beginning to pay rent. You'll need to negotiate the length of this period and the conditions.

Renewal Option: Sometimes during the lease point negotiations, your tenant might try to negotiate an option to renew per negotiated rates at the end of the lease. For the tenant, this is a calculated bet that the market will trend higher than the negotiated lease renewal rates. For you, it's an opportunity to nearly guarantee the same tenant will be in the building if you think rates won't go up much, if at all. Ideally, you'll want to stay away from renewal options, but it's understandable why a tenant would want them, especially if he or she has made a sizable investment in time and money for improvements in the space.

Condition of Space at End of Lease Term: Generally, any improvements the tenant makes to the space will be the property of the owner at the end of the lease term. If the improvements are minor or common, they can usually be carried over to the next tenant. However, if the improvements are highly specialized, you'll probably want them removed by the tenant before move-out. This is something you'll need to negotiate prior to the lease signing.

Holdover Penalties: If your tenant comes to the end of the lease and has either not moved out or negotiated a new lease, you'll want to make sure you have a clause in the contract that penalizes the tenant as an inducement to make sure a new lease is promptly negotiated or that tenant moves on. Generally, you'll want to charge 125 to 150 percent over the rental rate as an incentive to either move on or re-up.

USE

Because there are many different types of commercial real estate, the use clause of a lease sets the standard for the type of business and operations that can be conducted in your building. Obviously, as the owner, you'll want to make sure the business fits the zoning and structure and the building is not abused or stretched in some way beyond its intended use. For instance, you wouldn't want a chemical processor setting up shop in an anchor building of a retail development.

Your tenant, on the other hand, will want as much flexibility as possible to conduct business and pursue profits. Because of this, a tenant might even try to negotiate that you can't rent to competitors as part of the use clause.

When negotiating the use clause of the lease, you'll want to do your homework to make sure your building meets all the zoning laws for the type of business and tenant that is moving in. If there are any guarantees in the lease regarding zoning, you don't want an unexpected permitting or zoning violation to come up and cause possible legal issues between you and your tenant. Conversely, you'll want to make sure there is a clause in the contract that indemnifies you from any legal ramifications if your tenant knowingly breaks zoning and permitting laws without your knowledge.

Finally, make sure there's a clause stipulating that the tenant is not to do any illegal business or activities. You don't want to be legally liable for the meth lab you didn't know existed.

SECURITY DEPOSIT

One of the great things about real estate is, unlike other types of investments, you can insure it. What about your lease? While there isn't, technically, lease insurance, there is something you can use to insure yourself against potential losses from a poor tenant: the security deposit. While it won't be enough to cover all your losses, having a security deposit on hand does take the edge off if things get screwy.

The size of the security deposit will depend on varying market conditions, but, generally, at least one month's rent is a good starting point. Obviously, if you can get it higher, do. The amount should be enough that your tenant will be very concerned about recouping it.

Once you've decided on the amount of the security deposit, there are a few items you'll need to nail down regarding the deposit itself.

First, you'll want to detail when the deposit is due. You may negotiate to have all the deposit paid at the lease signing, or you may allow the tenant to pay a portion for a certain number of months until paid in full.

You'll also want to define the conditions upon which the deposit will be returned—or not returned, should that be the case. This is something many standard form leases don't do. But you can imagine the trouble of a he-said-she-said scenario regarding the return of the deposit money. It's always a good policy to have these things in writing and signed off on.

The lease should also define when the deposit is due back to the tenant upon move-out. Generally, this will be thirty days after move-out. You'll want to make sure the lease also defines that the deposit is refundable and not a last-month's rent, or else you'll have to pay taxes on it.

TENANT IMPROVEMENTS

As discussed earlier in the book, part of the negotiations for a lease will cover tenant improvement conditions for the tenant's space. Again, depending on the market, you'll want to determine who will be paying for what and how much.

Beyond responsibility for improvement costs, however, there are other matters to consider in regard to tenant improvements. For one, you'll want to maintain as much control over the improvement process as possible. This means you'll want to make sure the lease stipulates that the tenant must submit plans to you for approval and that you won't be financially responsible for payments to contractors working on your property.

You'll also want to make sure that while the improvements are underway you do not want to disturb other tenants and block doorways, passageways, stairways, and more.

Here's a list of common provisions you'll want to make sure are in your contract regarding tenant improvements:

Lien Protection: In most cases, if a general contractor is paid but doesn't pay his sub-contractors, those sub-contractors can file a lien against the property, which encumbers it and makes it impossible to sell or refinance until the lien is paid. You'll want to make sure that you have provisions in the contract that protect you from liens. In some states, you can negotiate a no-lien contract with a general contractor, which all sub-contractors will also be bound to. If that's so, you'll want to make sure that type of contract is required by your lease agreement. In the case where that type of contract isn't available, you'll want to make sure your lease requires a bond of some sort by the tenant to cover any potential losses.

Required Investments: In a particularly good owner's market, you can sometimes stipulate that the tenant complete required improvements to the space such as work to enhance the space. This could include work to enhance building efficiency, better building standard entry doors or upgraded mini blinds. If you're able to negotiate these types of things, they are a great way to get improvements to your investment without going out of pocket. If you do have a clause like this, make sure to negotiate the ability to review all plans and work before final completion.

To Whom the Alterations Belong: Make sure any improvements to the space belong to you upon move-out. You wouldn't want the tenant stripping the space and leaving a shell.

Tax Implications of Improvements: If the tenant makes significant improvements to the space, it's likely your taxes will go up when the assessor issues an occupancy permit. You'll want some sort of clause in the lease that adjusts the tenant's share of taxes, should this occur.

COMMON AREA MAINTENANCE

In most buildings there will be common areas that need maintaining. As an owner, you don't want to be responsible for these costs since they benefit your tenants. It's important to have provisions in the lease that make the tenants responsible for the common areas and the associated maintenance costs. The following are a few things to keep in mind when discussing common area maintenance:

Definition of floor area: When you define the floor area of the tenant's leased property, you'll want to make a pro-rata share of the common areas part of the contract, which will be the basis for costs passed on to the tenant. If you build more space and common areas on your property, the tenant will want a provision that will allow for a redraft of the common area budget based on the new space and square footage.

Maintenance charges: These costs will vary depending on the occupancy of the building. If there are fewer people occupying the building, things like utilities will be lower. If there are more people, they will be higher. At the heart of the negotiations will be the idea of a base year. What will be the standard by which costs will be negotiated? If you execute a lease with a tenant when your building is 50 percent occupied, it may not be beneficial for your base year to reflect that occupancy. When the building fills up, you may lose some income based on complicated base year income. Conversely, your tenant doesn't want full occupancy to be the base year either, as he or she will pay more than a fair share in costs. Once you negotiate the base year, you'll then want to make sure there are provisions for increases each year.

Janitorial Service: Often, the landlord will provide a janitorial service as part of the lease. You'll want to have this in the lease, determine who pays for this, and stipulate the days on which the service will be available.

Trash: Refuse costs are generally part of the common area costs. However, if you have a tenant that creates excessive amounts of trash, you'll want to negotiate a clause requiring that tenant to arrange and pay for additional trash management services.

Parking: Parking is a big deal. The tenant is concerned with making sure there are enough spaces not just for the business's employees but for its clients, and that those spaces are not too far away from the offices. In many cities, there are regulations on how many spaces per square feet are required. In older cities, there are many buildings that may have much lower ratios. In newer areas, there is plenty of land, and newer zoning laws might allow for a plethora of spaces. Basically, the parking headache will vary for each situation. Things to negotiate will be the number of spaces per leased space, whether those spaces are for exclusive use to the tenant or not, whether they are covered or not, how close they are to the building, the security provided to protect the cars parked, and, if you're smart, the cost per month for those parking spaces.

Signage: Signs can be a blessing or a curse. They can create and enhance business, or they can detract from the value of a property by marring the exterior. As the landlord, you'll want to control the signage, not just for aesthetic reasons but also to make sure that all signage complies with local municipal signage laws. Make sure to have provisions in the lease that require the tenant to submit design plans for the signage and that stipulate that the tenant cannot put up any signage unless it's approved by you and is properly permitted.

INSURANCE

The ability to insure real estate is a significant advantage of real estate investment over other types of assets, but insurance does cost money. Thankfully, you should be able to negotiate that your tenants cover the cost of insurance in most cases.

You'll want to make sure, as part of the condition of leasing, that your tenants must purchase a policy that, at the minimum, covers the cost of your mortgage. You'll also want them to have coverage that indemnifies you and the property against any damages that occur as a result of their business operations. You don't want to get sued if your tenants do something that hurts someone through no fault of your own.

DEFAULT AND SUBLETTING

One of the harsh realities of life is that businesses fail or at least hit hard times that change their financial landscape. Even if you do all your homework and pick the best tenant, there's always a chance the tenant will not be in a position to honor the lease. In such a case, the tenant will have two options: default or sublet.

In the case of a sublet, you'll want to make sure you've negotiated as much control over that process as possible. Otherwise, you'll be stuck with the possibility of having almost anyone move in—and a bad tenant can turn a good building into a nightmare. Make sure the lease is clear that any potential sub-letter must go through the same vetting process as the original tenant—and that you control that process.

In the case of default, you'll want sufficient provisions in the lease to compensate you for the loss in the form of cancellation fees and late fees as well as interest on past-due monies, retained security deposits, and other measures.

SALE OR REFINANCE

When it comes time to sell or refinance a property, the leases on hand determine the value of your property. As such, any leases you negotiate must be transferrable to another owner and/or lender. If they aren't, you'll be unable to sell or refinance. In addition to making the leases transferable, if you're selling the property, you'll want to make sure any lease has provisions that release you from any personal responsibility to the lease provisions once the building is sold and has changed hands.

YOU NEED A TEAM

If all the information in this chapter seems a little overwhelming, it's because it is. Each one of these points could be whole chapters in a book, and many people go to school for years to learn the ins and outs of negotiating lease deal points.

My purpose here is not to give you a comprehensive knowledge of negotiating these deal points but rather to give you a working knowledge so that you at least have a baseline from which to work.

I strongly suggest you put together a good team when it comes time to actually begin this process. Your team will consist of professionals who can advise you and bring their expertise to help you negotiate the best lease and protect you from any traps along the way.

At the minimum, I suggest having the following people on your team: broker, lawyer, architect, contractor, property manager, and engineer. You may not always need them for every deal, but you don't want to be searching for them when you're in the middle of negotiating one. Do your research now and build out the proper team.

The most important person on your team will be a solid leasing agent—naturally. Why? Because this agent will be the hub of your deal wheel. Your agent will handle interfacing with all your team members and give you the confidence of knowing that one person is committed to making sure every aspect of your deal is as perfect and as much in your favor as possible. A good leasing agent has a deep Rolodex, deeper knowledge, and the experience necessary to make your deal successful.

What makes a good leasing agent? That's what we'll talk about next.

CHAPTER 6

NINETEEN THINGS TO LOOK FOR IN A LEASE

I n the last chapter, we covered some of the basic elements of a lease that you'll need to negotiate. While it's important to understand those nuanced elements of a lease, it's also equally important to know some block and tackle elements you should be looking for in the lease itself when it comes time to sign on the dotted line.

There are some very basic terms that should be included in every lease document in order to protect you and to ensure clear expectations between you and your tenant. Remember, the Lease is a legal document. Therefore, you need to make sure all the negotiated deal points are covered and that the proper legal terms are covered to make sure the basic legal obligations are met.

The lease must include clauses covering items and instances that neither party hopes will happen. Over the years, I've learned that trusting good intentions is not good business. No matter how amiable you are with potential tenants, it's important to have a clear legal document in place. Even though neither party hopes that disputes will happen, conflicts can and, in my experience, often do occur.

A lease also allows you to have a clear roadmap for expectations, and provides a reference point for information. When starting out in this industry, a property manager once told me that her door was always open and that she would help with any questions I had. That being said, she told me to always first RTFL (**R**EAD **T**HE **F**LIPPING **L**EASE!) before coming into her office. I still use that advice today, and it still answers 99% of all my questions. Once you have the supporting evidence or information, you can then determine how you want to handle a situation.

The following are 19 elements that are key to have in your lease:

#1: BUILDING AND PREMISES

a. Building location: Include the address of the building, the building name, and suite location. It's also a good idea to attach a floor plan.

b. Condition of premises: You should specify if the tenant is accepting the premise in its "AS IS" condition on the Lease Commencement Date and whether or not you will be obligated to provide or pay for any improvements, work or services related to improvements, remodeling, or refurbishment of the premises.

c. Rentable Square Feet: The rentable square feet of the premises and the building should be subject to verification from time to time. This is usually an approximate number and you should have your building architect verify the actual square footage when you buy, or at a minimum when you lease, each space.

#2: DATE AND LEASE TERM

(Attach commencement letter if no hard date. A commencement letter is a letter sent to the tenant after they have moved in, confirming the commencement date of the lease.)

a. Date: Include date of lease execution.

b. Lease Term: To clarify the lease commencement date is important because it can differ from the lease execution date. If the commencement date is at the completion of tenant improvements, then you should attach a Commencement Letter as an exhibit to the lease, which should include the lease expiration date.

    In addition, if improvements will be completed prior to move-in, it's smart to state that the lease commencement date is either when the tenant starts business or the date that the premise is ready for occupancy, whichever is the earliest.

c. Commencement Letter: This form letter is usually attached to the Lease if a hard commencement date has not been established at the time of execution, i.e.: commencement date will be determined when tenant improvements are completed. When ready, the landlord will complete this form letter and send it to the tenant for execution. This is a separate action from executing the original lease. This establishes that both parties agree to when the lease and/or rent will commence and sets the expiration date for the lease. You should also include a time frame for how many days the tenant has to return an executed commencement letter.

#3:   BASE RENT AND ADDITIONAL RENT

This should include:

a. The monthly amount and tax

b. If and when the rent increases

c. To whom and where to send payments

d. If there is any rent abatement (rent the tenant doesn't have to pay, such as concessions)

e. The date that rent is due and also the date the rent is late

f. The amount that is due on the date of execution of the lease

g. If applicable, the tenant portion of the operating expenses (aka, additional rent) and their portion or percentage of those expenses

h. The tenant's base year, which establishes the maximum amount of expenses the owner will pay over the life of the lease per year. Any expenses in future years, which exceed this amount, are "passed through" to the tenant in addition to the rent.

#4: USE OF PREMISE AND BUILDING RULES

a. You should lease to a tenant whose business use is a good fit for your building and then make sure that they cannot change their use to something else that won't be a good fit.

b. Building Rules can include anything that is specific to your building, such as but not limited to:

i. Building hours

ii. Not allowing a tenant to change the locks without your approval

iii. Times you allow deliveries and if there is a specific elevator or area where deliveries can be made

iv. Whether or not animals are allowed in the building

#5: SERVICES AND UTILITIES

a. Include which services are included and when, such as:

   i. Janitorial services: typically allow for five days a week, except for nationally and locally recognized holidays, which are designated by the owner.

   ii. Elevators

   iii. City water from building outlets for drinking fountains, lavatory, and toilet purposes

   iv. Electrical wiring and power for normal, general use only

   v. Heating, ventilation, and air conditioning ("HVAC") when necessary for comfort during normal office use in the premises. Generally allow from Monday through Friday between 7:00 a.m. to 6:00 p.m. and on Saturday between 8:00 a.m. to 1:00 p.m., except for nationally and locally recognized holidays, which, again, are designated by the owner.

   vi. The cost if a tenant goes over the standard hours of service(s)

   vii. Also, include if there will be an administration fee or percentage and the amount for any additional services.

#6: REPAIRS

a. You should include items that a tenant is responsible to maintain and keep in good order and which items for which you will be responsible.

b. Indicate that, if the tenant fails to make needed repairs, you have the right to make them and that you can bill the tenant back for any of those repairs, which should include overhead and a percentage for your involvement.

#7: ADDITIONS AND ALTERATIONS

a. Your tenant should never be able to change anything to the suite or building without your written consent.

b. If you allow the tenant to construct their own improvements you should always have a right to vet their contractor and require the tenant to carry "Builders All Risk" Insurance.

c. The contractor must also provide insurance. The following types of insurance should be requested: Workers Comp, Employers Liability Insurance, Comprehensive General Liability, Auto Liability, and Umbrella/Excess Liability. A waiver of Subrogation should also be requested as well as requiring an actual Additionally Insured ENDORSEMENT that names not only you, but the Ownership/Entity and management company. Depending on the type of alterations, you will need to determine what limits will be acceptable.

d. If the tenant is paying the contractor directly, require your tenant to obtain a lien and completion bond, or some alternate form of satisfactory security in an amount sufficient to ensure the lien-free completion of the alterations. This security should name you as a co-oblige. Upon completion, tenant must provide a copy of the "as built" drawings of alterations and deliver evidence of payment with full and final waivers from Contractors and subs.

e. Indicate a fee to cover any out of pocket costs, legal review, architect review, and other supervision fees you may incur, including your own time.

f. Don't allow your tenant access to any of the building's equipment rooms without supervision.

g. Indicate that you expect the tenant to leave the additions and alterations or if you expect them to put the suite back to how it was prior to them. Also include if you expect the tenant to remove all their cabling, which I highly recommend because it is very hard to reuse and most vendors believe it is easier to run new cabling then to try and retrace what is currently there. If the tenant fails to remove the cabling, make sure you have the right to do so and bill tenant.

h. If you have agreed to specific tenant improvements prior to occupancy, a "Tenant work Letter" is typically attached as an exhibit. The work letter should outline if both the tenant and you have approved the constructions drawings and that if there are any alterations to the drawings that it will be at the expense of the tenant. This section should also include that the space is ready for occupancy upon substantial completion.

#8: COVENANT AGAINST LIENS

a. Include verbiage to protect yourself against liens that may be caused by a tenant. This is important, so make sure the tenant has no authority or power to cause or permit any lien or encumbrance of any kind whatsoever, and that any and all liens and encumbrances created by your tenant shall be attached to your tenant's leasehold interest only.

#9: INSURANCE / INDEMNIFICATION AND WAIVER

a. You should always require your tenant to carry insurance.

b. In this section of the lease, include how much and what type of coverage is required by your tenant, such as general liability, auto insurance, and workers comp.

c. You also want the tenant to indemnify you and carry a waiver of subrogation, meaning you won't be responsible for losses related to insurance subrogation.

#10: CONDEMNATION

a. In the event of condemnation, you need to be protected. If even a portion of the premises, building or real property, is taken by power of eminent domain or condemned by any competent authority for any reason, or if you grant a deed or other instrument in lieu of such events, you need to have the option to terminate the lease.

#11: ASSIGNMENT AND SUBLETTING

a. A tenant should never have the right to assign or sublet their space without your prior written consent.

b. If you are willing to consent, the tenant should remain fully liable for all obligations under the lease.

c. Make it a requirement to see the new potential tenant's financials and vet them in order to make sure it is a reputable company.

d. Your tenant should be responsible for all costs associated with the assignment and subletting, including all legal costs.

#12: SURRENDER OF PREMISES AND REMOVAL OF TRADE FIXTURES

a. The Surrender of Premises clause indicates that, no matter what you do, a tenant cannot just turn in their keys, surrender the premise, and terminate the lease without your written acknowledgement.

b. This section also should include that all personal property and all business and trade fixtures, machinery and equipment, furniture and movable partitions, which are not a part of the tenant improvements, and are owned or installed by the tenant at its expense, shall remain the tenant's property, and shall be removed by tenant at any time during the lease term as long as tenant is not in default.

c. Upon the expiration of the lease term the premises are returned to you in as good order and condition as when the tenant took possession, with an allowance for reasonable wear and tear.

d. Require the tenant to remove all telephone, data, and other cabling and wiring they installed (including any above the ceiling or below the floor), all debris and rubbish, and any furniture, equipment, free-standing cabinet work, and other articles of personal property owned, installed, or placed by tenant at its expense.

#13: HOLD OVER AND RATE

a. Hold over is when a tenant stays in the suite after the expiration of the lease term, with or without your consent, and goes to month-to-month status. Hold over doesn't constitute a renewal or an extension of the lease. It's not ideal because it creates financial uncertainty for you. If a tenant holds over without your consent, it may compromise or otherwise affect your ability to enter into new leases with prospective tenants regarding the Premises. To offset this risk, you should set a hold over rate equal to a large percentage over the rental rate during the last rental period of the lease term, usually somewhere from 100% to 200%.

#14: ESTOPPEL CERTIFICATES

a. Include a clause requiring the tenant to sign an estoppel certificate upon your request, which should include a time frame to return the document.

b. An estoppel certificate is designed to give third parties critical information on the relationship between your and your tenant. The third party is frequently either a prospective buyer or a lender that requires such certificates for use in a "due diligence" review of the property.

c. An estoppel certificate requires the tenant to certify that as of the date of the document certain things are true, such as:

   i. Whether the tenant's lease is in full force and effect and has not been assigned, modified, supplemented, or amended

   ii. Whether all conditions under the lease to be performed by the landlord have been satisfied

   iii. Whether any required contributions by the landlord to the tenant on account of the tenant's improvements have been received by the tenant

   iv. Whether there are any existing claims, defenses, or offsets that the tenant has against the enforcement of the lease by the landlord

   v. Whether any rent or related payment obligation has been paid more than one month in advance

   vi. Whether any security has been deposited with the landlord

d. Also in this section, you should require that at any time during the lease term, your tenant can be asked to provide you with a current financial statement and financial statements of the two years prior to the current financial statement year, and that these statements will be prepared in accordance with generally accepted accounting principles.

e. Failure of your tenant to timely execute and deliver estoppel certificates or other instruments should constitute an acceptance of the premises and an acknowledgment by your tenant that the statements included in the estoppel certificate are true and correct, without exception.

#15: SUBORDINATION

a. The subordination clause states that the lease is subordinate to any existing or future mortgages on the property. Thus, if you default on the mortgage and the lender forecloses, the lender has the right to terminate the lease and evict the tenant, even if the tenant has fulfilled all of its responsibilities under the lease.

b. If there is a mortgage on your property, the lender may actually require this clause.

#16: DEFAULTS / REMEDIES

a. Specify that nonpayment of rent or failure by the tenant to observe or perform any other provision of the lease constitutes a default, which, if it goes uncured, gives you the option to pursue one or more remedies.

b. Such remedies could include:

i. Terminating the Lease, in which event the tenant shall immediately surrender the premises to you.

ii. Terminating possession, where the lease continues in full force and effect (except for tenant's right to possess the premises) and the tenant continues to be obligated for and must pay all rent due under the lease.

#17: SECURITY DEPOSIT

a. Occasionally a security deposit is waived for tenants with outstanding credit, but it is always a good rule of thumb to include a security deposit.

b. The security deposit is usually equal to the last month's rent, but you can determine if it needs to be more or less. Checking a tenant's credit can help determine this.

c. You should specify what the security deposit can be used towards. Typically it is used for damages created by the tenant upon move out. However, if a tenant defaults and does not pay its rent, you should have the right to use it towards unpaid rent and the tenant should be responsible to restore the security deposit within a certain specified time frame.

#18: ENTRY BY LANDLORD

a. Make sure you always have the right to enter a premise, at reasonable time and upon reasonable notice, to:

   i. Inspect the property.

   ii. Show the property to prospective purchasers, mortgagees, ground lessors, or, during the last twelve months of the year, potential lessors.

   iii. Post notices of non-responsibility.

   iv. Complete alterations, improvements, or repairs if necessary to comply with current building codes or other applicable laws.

   v. Complete needed or deemed necessary structural alterations, repairs, or improvements to the building.

b. In addition, you should have the right to enter without notice to your tenant to perform janitorial and other services required of you by the lease.

#19: TENANT PARKING

a. Parking should never be taken lightly in a lease. Parking can provide extra income for you, make your building more or less marketable to tenants, and help with the resale of a building.

b. Make sure not to "over park" your building. A tenant with a parking requirement that is too high may not be the right fit for your building.

c. Typically, parking is given to a tenant on a per square foot basis, anywhere from 2.5 to 6 per thousand square feet.

d. If you do not know what the maximum parking per thousand square feet a tenant can receive, then I highly recommend you have a parking study completed.

e. In the lease, indicate if there is a cost for parking and if there are different rates for covered, uncovered, and reserved spots.

f. Also, indicate if the tenant will receive parking at no cost for a certain period of time and when they are expected to start paying.

Finally, I have found it useful, if not mandatory, to include a summary at the beginning of a lease that includes some of the basic lease information and where one can look for certain items in a lease. It can look something like the following:

Summary Of Basic Lease Information
TERMS OF LEASE

DESCRIPTION

1. Date as of: XX
2. Landlord: XX
3. Address of Landlord (Section xx):   XX
4. Tenant: XX
5. Address of Tenant (Section xx)   XX
6. Premises (Article x):

    6.1 Premises: Approximately XX rentable square feet of space located on the XX floor of the Building (as defined below), as depicted on Exhibit A attached hereto, known as Suite XX.

    6.2 Building: The Premises are located in the "Building" whose address is XXX

7. Term (Article x):

    7.1 Lease Term: XX months

    7.2 Lease Commencement Date: The earlier of (i) the date Tenant commences business operations in the Premises, and (ii) the date that the Premises are Ready For Occupancy (as defined in Exhibit D attached hereto), which Lease Commencement Date is anticipated to be XX, 2013 (the "Anticipated Lease Commencement Date").

    7.3 Lease Expiration Date: The date that is XX months after the Lease Commencement Date.

8. Base Rent (Article X):

Months of Lease Term	Annual Base Rent	Monthly Installment of Base Rent	Annual Base Rental Rate per Rentable Square Foot of the Premises
X- X*	XX	XX	XX
X- X			

*Subject to abatement during the first six (6) months of the Lease Term, as provided in Section 3.2 of the Office Lease.

9. Additional Rent (Article x):

    9.1 Base Year: Calendar year XX

    9.2 Tenant's Share of Direct Expenses: XX

10. Security Deposit (Article x):   XX
11. Number of Parking Spaces (Article x):   XX
12. Brokers (Section x):   XX

As you can see, there is a ton of information required in a lease. Having a great attorney, and a great broker is paramount in making sure these documents are accurate and complete. The lease is also the ultimate value creation for your asset. Be sure to pay attention.

CHAPTER 7

TEN THINGS TO LOOK FOR IN A GOOD LEASING AGENT

I hope, after what you've read so far in this book, you understand how much work commercial real estate leasing can be. In fact, you could say it's a full-time job, right? In a very real sense, you probably don't have time to do it, let alone do it as well as you'd like. This is especially true if you're trying to build a solid real estate investment portfolio, still hold down a full-time job, and balance a family—as many investors do.

So, this is the part of the book where I put some cards on the table and say it's important for you to find a good leasing agent to help you build a successful portfolio. I'm not saying to hire me, though you can if you want and we're a good fit. Rather, I'm simply making the case for finding a good, qualified leasing agent to help you wherever you live.

Why?

The goal of this book is to help you build wealth for a lifetime. Part of building wealth is building a great team. I believe firmly that I would not be where I am today without a great team to help me.

Simply put, I can't think of a successful—I mean *really* successful—commercial real estate investor who isn't either an agent or doesn't have a great agent in each investment market. I have agents in and outside my own firm who help me all the time. And I've engaged more than fifty different firms in my career for my own investments, if that tells you something.

Here's the other surprising thing: I've never heard of anyone moaning or complaining about having an agent. I've heard them moan and complain about having a particular agent, but never about the need to have one. Rather, over the years, the biggest complaint I've heard anyone express is, "I have to get a new agent."

Why would the most successful investors and business people in the world all have a commercial real estate agent, and do so happily? They understand the importance of having an expert and a trusted advisor on their team—and that time is money.

Since time is money, and picking a good agent is essential to maximizing your time and money, it follows that you should know how to find a good one.

To be completely honest, one of the biggest pet peeves in real estate is an owner who doesn't know what he or she should be looking for in a leasing agent. Most pick an agent who's the nicest person or who reflects what they want to hear. Others are simply lazy and pick the first option they come across to get the process out of the way.

Picking an agent to partner with you on your leasing deals is one of the most important decisions you'll ever make. As such, you should give it the proper time and devotion as you would for your most important business decisions. Picking the wrong agent is a recipe for disaster and will ensure that you won't be successful.

Essential to picking the right agent is knowing your property. For instance, if you have two, small, 1,000-square-foot spaces available, you would want to hire someone who deals regularly with those types of properties. In my office, for example, you wouldn't deal directly with me on those properties; you would hire one of my team members, potentially my runner.

Conversely, if you have a substantial portfolio with millions of square feet that needs leasing, you'd be dealing with me directly. You wouldn't want to have my runner handling the project since he wouldn't be at the professional level needed for that type of deal.

Additionally, many big brokers don't do much work in smaller markets. So you wouldn't want to waste a bunch of time trying to engage a national firm to work your small-town account. Chances are there are some great local brokerages with brokers who specialize in your smaller market that would be a much better fit.

On the same note, you don't want to hire a broker who specializes in industrial real estate to run the account for your retail portfolio. You want to find a good broker suited for your portfolio size and market who also specializes in retail real estate.

In the end, it's all about context.

Not All Agents Are the Same

The reality is, not all leasing agents are equal. Some agents—and they come in all shapes, sizes, and specialties—are more concerned about their business than yours, which, in my opinion, makes for bad business all around and even worse relationships.

As with any business, there are both good apples and bad apples when it comes to leasing agents. Just because you find a bad apple doesn't mean the whole barrel is bad. Just as you'd take your time, do your research, and choose carefully in making an investment decision, you must also do the same when choosing a leasing agent to help you maximize the value of your investment portfolio of commercial real estate.

Not every agent is great...but there are some truly great agents.

CHAPTER 7

THE BENEFITS OF A GREAT LEASING AGENT

A great leasing agent is the hub of your deal. The agent will be the touch point for all the moving parts and your go-to person for pretty much anything that needs to get done.

Need someone to review the contracts? Your agent will interface with you and your lawyer to help make sure your objectives are met and you understand every facet of the contract.

Need to find a good engineer to inspect a new tenant's improvements to a space? A good agent will know reputable folks to help you.

Need to fit three tours of your space into a day filled with task list, action items, and meetings? Your agent will take care of those tours for you.

Need to develop a comprehensive marketing plan to get a vacant space in one of your properties leased in between soccer games for the kids and that report due to your boss? Thankfully, your agent can handle that marketing plan for you.

Need access to top-notch market data? Your agent will have that all on hand and available at a moment's notice.

You get the point. Having a trusted agent and advisor can eliminate many of the tasks you simply won't have the time or potentially the expertise to handle yourself. The best part is, your agent will do these things at no cost up front. Agents make money only if you make money. So you know they're motivated to make a good deal happen.

At the end of the day, you have to evaluate how much your time is worth. Do you have the time to do all the legwork required to learn how to prospect, market, negotiate, and lease your property correctly? How about spending most of your free time putting that knowledge into practice and even risking making a costly mistake and having to rebuild from the ground up?

Or is it worth it to you to use your time to find a great partner in a leasing agent who can do these things for you at no initial cost and pay him or her out of the deal for the time and effort, saving you hundreds if not thousands of hours and dollars?

Most people opt for the latter, and my advice to you is to do the same.

ARE THERE EXCEPTIONS?

Maybe you're thinking you're the exception. You can handle all this work yourself. You don't need an agent to help you. You'd rather save the money. And maybe you don't trust agents—middlemen—to begin with. You don't need a leasing agent.

I'll come out and say that occasionally it's better to do your own work. This is especially true if you can't find the right agent to lease your specific vacant space. If you are the type of person who is never happy with the help you receive and would never build the trustworthy relationship that's required to work successfully with any kind of advisor; you're right—you're better off working alone.

Others of you might really like the idea of working with an agent. However, as a word of warning, not every deal and property will be best for contracting with an agent. For instance, smaller buildings and deals might provide so little return that they simply wouldn't be worth the time and effort an agent would have to put in for the return the deal would provide.

My advice in instances like this is to actually do some of your own legwork and use it as a foundation for bigger deals in the future that would be ideal for an agent. Use the experience as a learning opportunity to understand the industry better. The good news is, on smaller deals the time commitment is much less and the potential losses, if there is a mistake, are much smaller.

Even if you don't have a deal that's ready for a full-time commitment from an agent, I'd still encourage you to begin relationships with reputable agents. At the very least, most good agents will be happy to help you at no charge by providing some great market research and by getting you in contact with good folks who can help you with your deal, such as lawyers, inspectors, and more. Plus, when a bigger deal does come down the pipe, you'll have already begun the process of having trusted advisors waiting to help you build a successful deal.

So, now that I've laid the groundwork for why you should have a great leasing agent on your team, let me share with you the ten things you should look for in a good leasing agent.

#1: EXPERIENCE

This one is a no brainer. If you've learned anything from this book so far, it's that there are a lot of moving parts to commercial real estate leasing and that it can take years of full-time commitment to master the art. As such, it's important to entrust your investments to someone who has the proper experience to lease them well. It's one thing to try and do it on your own and make some mistakes. They're your mistakes! It's quite another to be the training wheels for someone else.

This is not to say you shouldn't work with young or up-and-coming agents. Always do so under the umbrella of an experienced and successful agent. I have a number of young agents in my firm who will be great someday. For now, I keep a close tab on what they're up to in order to make sure my clients are well served. Any agent you work with should have the same level of care for you.

#2: GOOD RAPPORT WITH YOU

Here's a thought: You have to actually get along with your leasing agent. You're going to be spending a lot of time with this person, so make sure there is compatibility between the two of you. There's nothing worse than dreading a phone call or a meeting with someone with whom you're supposed to be doing business. Eventually, if you're not careful, a bad relationship can turn into a toxic one, and then you're faced with poor performance and possibly the need to fire your agent.

Also, your agent should be genuinely concerned about making sure your needs and objectives are rightly understood. This means your agent will ask you questions, take notes, follow up, and generally be eager to help in any way. The sad reality is, there are a lot of commercial leasing agents out there who are concerned about themselves more than about their clients. Make sure your agent is more concerned about building a great relationship and rapport with you by focusing on making you a success instead of focusing on how much money he or she can make.

#3: DEAL MAKER VS. PROCESSOR (AGENT AND OTHER AGENTS)

Some leasing agents are milquetoasts. They get pushed around by other agents and don't actually represent their clients well. This can lead to a lot of frustration for you, the owner, as you continually are presented with offers that are well below your expectation.

This type of leasing agent is concerned more with processing a deal than with making one. It's easy to simply be the middleman and bring counter deal points to each party. It's quite another to know your client's objectives and goals and to fight for those objectives and goals in order to make sure you broker the best possible deal. The latter takes expertise, knowledge, persistence, courage, and a mastery of the art of leasing. The former is pure laziness, greed, and a lack of the true essence of how to lease commercial space.

Additionally, while you want your agent to be pushing other agents to make a deal happen that works for you and your objectives, you also don't want a "yes man" working for you. Acquiescing to your every demand without giving good counsel is the way of a processor who just wants to get the deal done instead of partner who is looking out for your best interests. You don't want a middleman. You want a partner who shares expertise and is genuinely concerned about making sure you get the best possible deal based on all the circumstances.

#4: VELOCITY OF WORK

In the world of commercial real estate, you have to move fast. There's no room for pushing your lead follow-up to another day. Those who are able to respond first are often the ones who win. That's why one of the most important factors in finding a good leasing agent is finding one who understands the importance of velocity of work. Here, I'll briefly share my standards for velocity of work at Lee & Associates. When you're looking to partner with a leasing agent, I encourage you to find someone who works similarly.

Responsiveness: When we get an inquiry from a broker, potential tenant, or client, we have strict standards in place to follow up. These are the baseline. Often, we follow up immediately. Our brokers are not to go any longer than the times listed, but they are certainly encouraged to move at a faster velocity.

- Every email is answered within two hours.

- Every phone call is returned within four to six hours.

- Any other form of inquiry is also answered within four to six hours.

Interest: When you've done the hard work of leasing, you don't want the deal to fall apart because you drag your feet in being responsive to interest shown in your property. When offers and letters of intent come in, my firm has the following policies in place.

- We make counter offers within twenty-four hours.

- We happily take the prospect around the area and do follow-up tours with them as soon as possible.

- We follow up consistently, calling regularly to make sure counters have been received and to push for action.

Also, as soon as a deal is agreed upon, we push the teams working on the deal to finish up the contract and build-out phases as quickly and efficiently as possible. After all, time kills all deals, and we're here to get leases signed, not to be timid. At the end of the day, this creates great deals in reasonable timelines and helps avoid deals falling apart.

#5: REPUTATION

While it's true that you want to find an agent who is experienced, you will also want to find one with a good reputation. There are successful people in this world with whom I would rather not do business because of their reputation. I'm sure you've met people you feel the same way about. Sometimes this isn't even because of bad things like crooked deals; it could also be due to something as simple as an extreme personality conflict that would make it difficult to have a good rapport.

Before you engage a new agent, ask for references and also do some sleuthing of your own to get an idea of how that person does business and what it's like to interact with him or her, and, most importantly, to determine that past business was done with the utmost integrity.

#6: COMMITMENT TO WORKING YOUR PROJECT

This seems simple, but hiring a broker who wants to work your building is crucial. You're looking for a broker who is committed to your project, will work on cold calling, will invest in marketing, and spend time showing it. Often this person is hard to find. Make sure you don't settle on a broker until you have found the one who will work hard for you.

#7: MINDSET THAT'S BASED ON RELATIONSHIPS, NOT TRANSACTIONS

Some agents are all about the money. They care a lot about the deal and very little about the people who make the deal possible. As such, they develop a transaction-based mindset that is unhealthy for long-term success and often not in your best interest. These are the types of agents who will do anything to make a deal work so they can collect a commission. Very often, they'll sacrifice a long-term relationship for a short-term gain and simply move on to the next client and the next deal. The problem is, after a couple years of this behavior, they effectively black-list themselves. Because they have a poor reputation, both potential clients and other agents simply won't work with them or will make working together very difficult.

Good leasing agents are first and foremost relationship-based. They have your interests above theirs, making sure to take care of you in hopes of building a long-term relationship that will benefit both them and you for many years to come. Additionally, most good deals come out of relationships between brokers. So it's important that your agent has a good relationship not only with you but also with the broader commercial real estate brokerage community.

#8: ACCESS TO DECISION MAKERS

Another big reason for partnering with an experienced leasing agent is the access you gain to his or her Rolodex. While you may struggle to make contact with the owner of a company or the decision-making VP in a large corporation, a good leasing agent will have direct access to such people and possibly even a good relationship or friendship to draw on. This is a huge advantage when you're trying to lease your building. Your agent can get the blood in the water many times faster than the average person with no access to decision makers.

#9: LOCATION KNOWLEDGE

If you've been investing in Phoenix, Arizona, and you've decided to start investing in Dallas, Texas, as well, it won't do you any good to ask your leasing agent in Phoenix to help you lease your buildings in Dallas. Why? Part of what makes a great leasing agent is in-depth knowledge of a specific area. This knowledge includes market data as well as a deep reservoir of relationships to draw from in an effort to lease your building to the best possible tenant.

Commercial real estate seems like a big world, but it's actually a number of small, tightly knit, local ecosystems. Each time you enter a new ecosystem, you'll need to seek out and find good team members who are part of that ecosystem to help you structure your deals and make them successful. This includes a good leasing agent. In my personal investments, I have hired and worked with more than fifty different real estate companies (and a lot more agents). Most of these involved deals for which I needed a good agent in a specific market other than my own.

#10: SPECIFIC TRANSACTION-TYPE KNOWLEDGE

Each different type of commercial real estate requires its own knowledge set. If you're planning on focusing on investing in industrial real estate, you'll want to partner with an agent who also specializes in industrial. The same with retail, office, and more.

Also, as there are various classes of commercial real estate (classes A, B, and C), some agents are better suited to help you lease class A properties while others excel at class C properties. Each class takes a different skill set to interact with a different type of client. As important as it is to determine what type of investor you are and what type of properties you invest in, it's equally important to make sure your agent is a good match for you and your portfolio profile.

CHAPTER 8

WHERE TO FIND A GOOD LEASING AGENT

N ow that you know what to look for in a good leasing agent, you may be wondering where to look for one. Let me give you a couple of quick ideas.

Word of Mouth: Probably the best way to find a good agent is to talk with other people. Ideally, if you're in the real estate investment business, you're networking with other investors and service providers in your industry. This means you have a wealth of knowledge from which to draw. All you have to do is ask! This is true even if you're going into a new market where you don't know anyone. Chances are, someone in your existing network knows someone in that city who knows someone in that city who knows a great leasing agent. You get the idea. Leverage your contacts.

Drive the Market: You want an expert, right? Drive the submarket. By this I mean see who has posted signs and who is leasing space in their projects (new construction, new changes to the directory, etc.), and call the agents on those signs.

Call Out-of-Market Buddies: Here's a tip I use all the time. I go to a submarket that's not mine and find the absolute best agent in that market. I then call the agent to see whom he or she would recommend for my project. Usually, I get two to three names. Then I go to another submarket and do the same. Once you get name of the same agent from two top projects, call that agent.

TAKE YOUR TIME AND CHOOSE WISELY

At the end of the day, choosing the right commercial real estate leasing agent is one of the most important decisions you'll ever make. So take your time and choose wisely. You'll have a lot of money riding on this relationship, and a lot of personal time and energy. It's important you trust that your agent has your best interests in mind and that you can build a long-term business relationship that is mutually beneficial.

CONCLUSION

WHAT IT WILL TAKE

We began this book talking about art and how it relates to commercial real estate leasing. So it seems only fitting that we end the book in the same way.

All artists have something in common. Painters start with paint, brushes, and a canvas. Musicians start with notes and instruments. Writers start with a blank piece of paper (or a blank computer screen, nowadays) and words. Baseball players start with a bat, a ball, and a glove.

The equipment and tools an artist needs to make a masterpiece are available to anyone who wants them. Yet very few make a masterpiece. Most aspiring artists, using the same tools and equipment available to all, make mediocre work that appeals to some but not many. Why?

The answer lies in the fact that great artists have something in common that others don't—they know how to use common elements to make something uncommon, how to take the ordinary and create the extraordinary.

In my career, I've helped facilitate more than 2,000 commercial leases, and each one was a work of art in its own way. By that, I mean each one had the same common elements talked about throughout this book, but those elements were brought together to form something unique and suited for all parties involved in that particular transaction.

As there is no standard lease, each one requires the skill of an artist to take the elements on hand and craft something original and as close to perfect as possible for the situation at hand.

THE BUILDING BLOCKS OF SUCCESS

My promise to you was that this book would teach you the following foundational building blocks of commercial real estate leasing:

- What leasing is and why it's important.
- How to position your building to be as attractive as possible.
- Why leasing really is marketing.
- How to be a better salesperson.
- The skills required to negotiate leases and evaluate offers.
- How to find and partner with the best team members.

Each of these has a chapter or more devoted to it, and I haven't held back anything I've learned along the way. Represented in these pages are years of trial and error, lessons from the proverbial school of hard knocks.

But I also promised that these things alone wouldn't be enough to make you great at leasing. They'll just get you started. To master the art and become successful, you must have "it." Only experience can teach you that.

YOU CAN DO THIS

What I do know, however, is that you can discover your "it," and you can move to the next level. Each and every one of us has the capacity for greatness inside ourselves. We are made for success, but sometimes we don't realize that success because of circumstances, both inside and out.

Some people have harder circumstances to overcome than others, but I'm a firm believer that anyone can surmount life's obstacles and become successful in anything they're passionate about.

Over the years, I've found that those who are able to achieve great things have shared certain qualities that allowed them to incrementally grow into the person they desired to be and to find their "it." Those qualities are:

Patience: The ability to put in the time required and not give up.

Passion: The ability to put your very best into every step of the journey.

Commitment: The ability to plan for success and execute that plan each day.

Tenacity: The ability to not give up in the face of adversity.

Honesty: The ability to know where you need help—and ask for it.

If you develop and continually build upon these qualities in your life, I know for a fact that you can do great things, both in the art of commercial leasing but also in so many other things as well.

Let's explore these qualities a little more.

THIS WILL TAKE PATIENCE

To reiterate what I said at the beginning of the book, there's no such thing as an overnight success. Rather, the most successful people in the world are those who bring to their craft a deep sense of passion, tenacity, and commitment. They go beyond the norm and give extraordinary effort to master their chosen field; practice in chunks, repeatedly; and learn from mistakes.

When I first started out in this business, I had a lot to learn and it took the help of those who'd already created great leases to help me understand the "chunks" I needed to work on. I had to take the time to learn research, marketing, selling, negotiating, and more, which allowed me the room to do so repeatedly, and to guided me through the many mistakes I made.

Just as new brokers-in-training in my firm spend three years in preparation to take the field as part of the team, it took years of hard work on my part, and investment from pros in my career, to be successful today.

If you've read through this book; understand the passion, tenacity, and commitment it takes to master the art of commercial real estate leasing; and are ready to begin your journey to reach that goal, my advice is: Be ready for a lot of hard—but fun—work over many years.

THIS WILL TAKE PASSION

Becoming successful in this business takes passion. It's not enough to put in the time—you have to care about what you are doing.

There are many actions we take in life that are time-consuming but that we skim through or do the least amount of work required to "get through it." Anyone who's asked a kid to clean a room knows this is true. Most kids will do the bare minimum, often cutting corners, in order to get the task done. Clothes, whether dirty or not, get stuffed into the hamper. Toys are shoved under the bed or haphazardly into toy bins. Bed sheets and covers are pulled into what remotely resembles a made bed. Kids are anything but passionate about cleaning their room! What ends up happening is more work is made, as the child is required to go back and redo the shoddy work until it is done properly.

I've never met them, but I'm sure there are a few kids out there who are passionate about a clean room. Maybe they hate clutter or are a bit OCD. For whatever reason, they love to have a clean room. I guarantee those rooms are meticulous; dare we say, a work of art. There's no dust anywhere. Clothes are folded and put away neatly. Toys are ordered by type, size, color, and year purchased. Somewhere, I'm sure this exists—and it's a testament to the difference passion can make in work.

In order to be the best at leasing that you can be, it will take passion. If you're not ready to dive in with all you have, to devote significant portions of your time, talent, and energy toward mastering it, then what's the point? You'll simply cut corners and do shoddy workmanship—and you might cost yourself a lot of money in the process.

THIS WILL TAKE COMMITMENT

You need to be in it to win it when it comes to leasing. If you don't plan on becoming great at leasing or it's just a task or process that you want to get out of the way, then you shouldn't do it. If you're passionate about the art of leasing, then be ready to commit to it, and to learn and develop your skills for a lifetime.

This is why we require such a long training program at Lee & Associates. Partly, we want to make sure our associates are trained well, but we also want to see if they have the ability to commit to something over the long-haul and bring passion to the table day in and day out—even on the most menial of tasks. We care about providing the highest level of service to our clients, and the last thing we want is an associate who isn't really passionate or committed to leasing to take the playing field and give half an effort or quit when the going gets tough.

Leasing isn't a hobby. It's a career and a calling. Treat it as such.

THIS WILL TAKE TENACITY

I do a lot of athletic training. Inevitably, there comes a time during training when your body is screaming for you to give up. You might have come to the exercise with passion and commitment, but adversity and opposition are begging you to quit. That's when you need tenacity to carry you through to your second wind. More than just commitment, tenacity is the quality to keep going and stay committed even in the face of the most difficult of circumstances.

There will be many things that cause you to want to quit. Sometimes, it will be failure. Other times, it will be other opportunities that seem more appealing at the time. Still other times, it will be others speaking negatively into your life. Whatever the source of your feelings to quit, only tenacity will carry you through to the finish line.

BE HONEST

If, at the end of this book, you know you lack the time, passion, commitment, and tenacity to master the art of commercial real estate leasing…that's OK. No one is saying you should or even need to lease your own properties. You have to be honest with yourself—because deceiving yourself into thinking you can "take a run" at this or "give it a shot" is a recipe for disaster.

If this book has taught you anything, I hope it's that you shouldn't do anything in life half-heartedly, including leasing. Rather than waste energy and time doing things you aren't passionate about, double down on those things you are passionate about, master them, and become as successful as you can be.

Everything else? Find a partner to accomplish those types of tasks for you—someone who has put in the time to master it, is passionate, is committed, and who exemplifies tenacity.

When it comes to commercial real estate leasing, this means you might be better served by seeking out the best possible partner for your properties in the form of a leasing agent. Thankfully, this book will help you have a great foundation to begin a dialogue with your leasing agent, and, thanks to the last chapter, you know what to look for and how to find one.

Whether you plan on doing your own leasing or finding someone to help you, you must be honest with yourself in order to be successful.

At the end of the day, whether you or a professional leases your property, I hope you understand the importance of making sure your properties have the best possible leases, because, as we've discussed, the value of your properties is dependent on the quality of your leases. Remember, you make your money on the lease—not just the buy.

The good news is you now know what is required to make sure your properties are leased well. This puts you light years ahead of most property owners. Now, it's up to you to make sure it happens.

Thanks for letting me be part of the beginning of your leasing journey. Here is your opportunity—your opportunity to be a great artist at this craft. This is just the beginning. Go and grow. Best of luck as you explore the art of commercial real estate leasing.

ABOUT THE AUTHOR

R. Craig Coppola is the top producing office broker in Lee & Associates' 35 year history, as well as one of the Founding Principals of Lee & Associates Arizona. He has completed over 3,500 lease and sale transactions over the past 30 years, totaling a value in excess of $3,500,000,000. Craig is among the very few—less than 40 worldwide—who has earned the top three designations in the real estate industry: CCIM, CRE and SIOR.

Craig served as NAIOP Chapter President of the Year in 2003, the highest personal honor given by the largest real estate development trade association (National Association of Industrial and Office Properties). In addition, he has been awarded NAIOP's office broker of the year six times. Craig is also a Past Chairman of the Southwest Chapter of CRE (Counselors of Real Estate). CRE is a trade organization representing the finest real estate consultants for over 50 years.

The Art of Commercial Real Estate Leasing is Craig's second book. *How to Win in Commercial Real Estate Investing*, his first book, was published April of 2014.

A third generation Arizonan and father of four remarkable children, Craig holds a Bachelor's Degree in Finance from Nicholls State University and a Master's Degree in Business Administration from Arizona State University. He and his wife are active within the Phoenix community and Craig is a sought-after national speaker on real estate and motivational topics.

INDEX

A

The ABC's of Property Management, 8
Absolute triple net lease, 15, 77
Absorption rates, 48, 49
Additions and alterations, 96, 97
Agents. *See also* Brokers
   benefits of good, 110, 111
   relationship with, 111–117
   reputation of, 115–116
   selection of, 107–117
   what to look for in, 107–117
   when not to use, 106–108
   where to find, 119–120
Amenities, 23, 31, 40, 62
Americans with Disabilities Act (ADA),
   24, 63
Analysis, market, 46–57
Anchor stores, importance of, 24
As is, 114
Asset classification, 29
Asset versus liability, 7–8
Assignment, 98

B

Background checks, 68
Best Buy, 69
Brochures, 43, 44
Broker open houses, 43, 57
Brokers, 55, 104. *See also* Agents
Building Owners and Managers
   Association (BOMA), 64
Building rules, 94
Buildings
   classification of, 29
   drive-by guide, 33–35

evaluating strengths/weaknesses,
   25–26, 35–41
importance of knowing, 25–26
information form about, 30–32
location of, 12–13, 24, 30
neighborhood evaluation, 33–35
quality of, 29, 40
two-story retail/office, 23–25
valuation of, 20–21
Business-to-business marketing, 42, 44
Business-to-consumer (B2C) market,
   41–43
Buying, versus leasing, 6

C

Canvassing, 57
Capitalization rate (cap rate), 19–20, 22–
   25, 49
Cash flow, 6–7, 12, 19, 22, 68, 75
Census Bureau, 50
Chambers of Commerce, 50
Class A/B/C properties, 15, 29, 117
Client interaction, 8, 54
Cold-calling, 8, 42, 57
Commencement letter, 92–93
The Commercial Lease Guidebook, 76
Commercial real estate
   versus residential, 13–14
   types of, 14, 26–29
Commitment, from agents, 111–112
Common area maintenance, 85–86
Company history, gathering, 68
Comparables, 48
Compromise, 75, 99
Concessions, 16–17, 19, 22, 47–49, 60–62,
   81, 93

INDEX

S

Sales
    client needs, 66–67
    cold-calling, 50, 68–69
    deal makers/breakers, 70–75
    evaluating proposals, 75–81
    tips for success, 81–84
SalesDogs, 64
Sales training, 9–11
Security deposit, 17, 83, 88, 100, 102
Self-storage units, 28
Services, included in a lease, 95
Signage, 43, 62, 66, 87
Singer, Blair, 54
Space planning, 24
Spec-suite program, 43
Stores, 51
Strengths and weaknesses analysis, 26, 35–36, 39–41, 60
Structural differences, affecting leases, 15
Subletting, 88, 98
Subornation clause, 101
Subrogation, waiver of, 96–97
Surrender of premises clause, 98–101

T

The Talent Code, 2
Target, 24
Taxes, negotiation of, 17, 78
Teams, used to negotiate, 9, 46
Tenant improvements (TI), 18, 29, 41, 44, 47, 55, 61, 75, 80, 93, 96–100
Tenant property tax, 14, 78
Tenant rosters, 42
Tenant work letter, 96–97
Termination, 47
Timeline, 39, 44–45
Training programs, 9–11, 58
Triple net lease, 14, 15, 77
Two-story retail/office buildings, 23–24

U

Urban Land Institute, 50
Use clause, 82–83
Utilities, who will pay, 14, 17, 19, 31, 64, 76–80

V

Vacancy rates, 26, 49–50
Valuation, of property, 20, 64
The Velocity of Work, 58, 114–115

W

Waivers, 96–97
Walmart, 24
Weakness, analysis of, 40–41
Will, George F., 1
Word of mouth, 119

Z

Zoning laws, 13, 83, 87